T0195717

One Acre
and
Insecurity

A Single Parent's Account

Lara Bonnell

WESTBOW
PRESS®
A DIVISION OF THOMAS NELSON
& ZONDERVAN

WestBow Press books may be ordered through booksellers or by contacting:

WestBow Press
A Division of Thomas Nelson & Zondervan
1663 Liberty Drive
Bloomington, IN 47403
www.westbowpress.com
1 (866) 928-1240

ISBN: 978-1-9736-0243-9 (sc)
ISBN: 978-1-9736-0244-6 (e)

Library of Congress Control Number: 2017914155

Print information available on the last page.

WestBow Press rev. date: 10/04/2017

DEDICATION

This is an "Irish account" (slightly exaggerated to lend a touch of humor to some basically impossible situations) of my years as a single parent with four teenagers. Since there were four adolescents and only one of me, they had to pitch in and help us survive as a family.

We still couldn't have made it without much prayer, a host of colorful friends plus supportive colleagues at River City College and my church. I hope this retelling of some very traumatic and crazy years will lend hope, perspective, and perhaps companionship to the many other single parents who would quit if they could, but who have no choice but to slog ahead amid the disarray of dreams for themselves and their offspring while fending off impending bankruptcy.

This book is dedicated to the four participating survivors who have gone on to college and solid careers despite their mother's often unorthodox and answer-to-prayer-at-wits-end parenting methods:

Susan, Ron, Martha and Patty.

Contents

CHAPTER ONE

Becoming a Single Parent

Like most single parents, I had not planned to be one. True, the children were always my idea. Having been raised as the oldest of four, I could hardly imagine a marriage without offspring. But the medical student I married was the younger of two, a much older sister completing their family. He observed that making ends meet while he was still in medical school in Cranston would be difficult enough without having kids. I would have to be content with a cat.

I kept explaining to four-footed Molly, "No kids, no kittens!" when she'd go into heat yowling and grotesquely rolling around. In our fourth-floor walkup apartment in a condemned building catty-corner across from Cole County Hospital, our cat had a litter box in the non-functioning fireplace screened off for her privacy. If we did go outside with Molly, she was on a short leash which she despised.

But one day she did manage to squeeze by me when I answered the door to a salesman. She zoomed down the four flights of steps, conned another tenant checking on mail to open the outer door, and wasn't seen for two days despite several searches by this frantic owner. When Mollie reappeared, she was battered and bleeding—as anxious to return to our apartment as she'd been to leave it. Later we did have three tiger-striped kittens resulting from that adventure. Since Molly was an orange tabby, I surmised that the father must have been tiger-striped. However, I was jealous…no kids, but three kittens for which to find homes.

"Be patient," advised my spouse. "I have to serve two years in the Army after interning. We can have a kid at government expense then if you and my folks are still so set on our having a baby."

Despite having graduated with honors from the University of

Indiana in English Teacher Training, I was working as an editor of reports for the Metallurgy Department of the Research Foundation at Cranston Institute of Technology. (In those days, if you weren't a graduate from Cranston Teachers College, you must be a substitute teacher for two years before being assigned to a regular classroom.)

My husband seldom came home, although spouses were permitted to join their mates for Sunday dinner at the hospital cafeteria. Each Saturday I'd take the El (elevated railway) downtown with a suitcase full of books to return to the Cranston Public Library in exchange for the next week's reading supply. After lunch at a Chinese restaurant I'd head for my one extravagance, a dance lesson at the Murray Dance Studio.

Eventually I earned a bronze medal there, the lowest rung of the ballroom dancing ladder. It was a nod to my childhood dream of becoming a graceful ballerina. This ambition was a source of great hilarity for my family since I was awkward, could fall up the stairs as well as down them, and had a knee that would occasionally lock and send me catapulting into hedges or onto lawns.

Having no partner for dancing, tennis or bridge meant that the Cranston years were lonely, solo ones. However, I very carefully calculated the months until my doctor husband would graduate and enter the Army. Susan was born in Austin, Texas on the same day Morgan reported for duty.

However, after ten years of marriage to that same medical student, intern, Army doctor, family physician, specialty resident, and Caring Clinic staff member, we were divorced. Although he did not consider I had enough "class" to match his new exalted and established status, I did have whatever was needed to have complete custody of our three children—Susan (age 6), Ronell or Ron (age 4) and Martha (almost 1 year).

Instead of alimony (being inexperienced and terribly proud), I asked for only enough funding to complete a master's degree within two years to be able to earn enough to support the kids and myself. I didn't want him running our lives. After all, I had given up the offer of a graduate fellowship to marry my medical student fiance on my graduation day. Another big and prideful error was limiting his child support payments to the minimum $50 per child per month required by Indiana law to guarantee his visitation rights plus two weeks each summer and an early Christmas every Thanksgiving Break. I could count on $150 per month in child support. He could claim all three children as dependents on his income tax, but to justify that, he would be responsible for dental, medical, and music or other lesson bills.

By the end of the first month after the divorce became final I realized that I should have listened to my lawyer and parents who had urged me to ask for much more. However, I stuck to the agreement, learning to economize and make do. After all, I had a small mortgaged house, a used car, and money enough for graduate tuition in Library Science at the University of Indiana, one of the best programs in the United States at that time. But every week, every month was financially tight.

Our two girls adjusted well, but young Ron was dealing badly with losing his dad and having to compete for attention with his baby sister. An apparently serious hip problem which meant he had to be carried around was finally diagnosed as psychosomatic. I took academic leave for a semester to lavish attention on my son and keep the baby as separate from him as I could.

Then along came a single Episcopal clergyman whom I'd known some years before and whose two churches were several counties north of Unity where we lived. He was invited to Martha's baptism at the University Episcopal Chapel along with other relatives and friends. I didn't know whether he felt sorry for us or just longed for a family, but in a few months and on the rebound I agreed to marry him if he could get his bishop's permission. I really doubted he could since divorce then was a scandal in the Episcopal Church, especially for clergy.

Don't tell me God doesn't have a sense of humor! Permission took twelve months and lots of paperwork. Meanwhile, the Bishop, after getting Fr. Patrick Sims' initial request, transferred him to St. James in Swerlin, a small mission church over on the eastern banks of the Mysterious River. It was the western outpost of the Diocese of Cranston. No doubt the Bishop hoped that the transfer and refusing to give a ruling for one year would make time and distance defeat our romance.

Patrick and I resolved the distance by my selling my home in Unity and moving to Dorian for a librarian's job with Northern Indiana University, about half way to Swerlin. Finally the Bishop gave us a dispensation and married us in Sampore in June, 1965.

We five crowded into the vicarage next door to St. James in Swerlin, and I taught school in Thornton, ten miles downriver. Sometime later I discovered that my second husband had only become a priest because he'd flunked out of law school in Halifax and not wanting to go home to Ripple, Ontario in disgrace, crossed the quadrangle and entered divinity studies in Halifax.

He also wanted to become a bishop and had noticed how most successful candidates had families. We four became Patrick's instant family. Many of my suppositions about rectory life like family devotions dwindled immediately to grace before meals. Every sermon somehow displayed his knowledge of New Testament Greek and Latin. We survived three attempts by disgruntled parishioners to have Fr. Patrick transferred.

I didn't want to admit I'd made another marital mistake, so I hung on for nine very long years and the birth of Patty. Susan was likely to graduate as valedictorian of her high school graduating class and I couldn't bring myself to rob her of that honor despite learning that Ron was being severely bullied in school and on his paper route.

I discovered Ron's problems when I noticed him packing his baseball bat with his newspapers before setting out on his paper route one afternoon.

"Are there bad dogs along your route?" I inquired, thinking he might need the bat if attacked by a ferocious canine.

"Not dogs, Mom...guys," he replied. This led to disclosures

of bullying at school and occasional incidents on his paper route. His doctor father insisted Ron be transferred to a private school for which he would pay. The closest private school, however, was ninety miles away in River City. To facilitate Ron's attendance, I applied for and obtained the post of Public Services Librarian and Archivist at River City College, a private four-year college.

For two years Ron and I commuted weekdays the180-mile round trip to River City which meant rising at 5 a.m. and heading to bed around 9 p.m. Then, in order that Ron could be on the basketball team, I took an apartment near the College and we only came home on weekends. Susan was old enough to prepare simple meals. She did graduate as valedictorian and headed off to the University of Illlinois for double majors in Performance Piano and Nursing.

Gradually during Susan's final high school year, Ron and I transferred all our belongings to the River City apartment. I consulted a lawyer in Mt. Crawford, the county seat, about requesting a divorce that summer. My lawyer was to call my husband on July 4th to explain why I had departed with all the children. Unbeknown to me, my lawyer was an alcoholic and was too drunk on July 4th to fulfill our agreed upon notice to Patrick. Instead I had to explain my personal Independence Day to Patrick myself in reply to his puzzled phone call.

By this time he was willing for me to leave, but he delayed legal proceedings until August and then fought successfully for primary custody of his daughter Patty. Since I already had custody of three children from a previous divorce, the judge granted his request with the proviso that Patty spend her weekends with me; Patrick and I would provide the necessary Friday night and Sunday evening transport on alternate weekends. "So much for ending the long commute," I thought.

I set a date to come and collect my piano from the vicarage. Our Siamese cat was delighted to see me again, but Patrick was determined to keep her to spite me. The only other possession he fought me for was the portable dishwasher…the one we'd argued long about needing and finally buying,

Financial division specified that Patrick would become sole owner of our cabin and land on Almighty Island where he was born and grew up. I was given the Swerlin bank stock. It seemed fair until I tried to cash the stock, only to discover it could not be redeemed for eight more years. Patrick's banker friend, however, advised me that he had an interested party who would purchase the stock for half its face valuc.

"You can tell Fr. Patrick that I'm keeping the stock and we'll manage until it expires," I told him indignantly and left. Anyway, I was legally single again and living in River City with Martha, Ron, Patty on weekends, and Susan on her academic vacations.

NOTE:

Eventually, after our divorce caused the Diocese of Cranston to order and pay for two years of weekly psychological counseling for my second husband, he was told that he'd never be placed in charge of a congregation again. He was not defrocked and could substitute and be paid for occasional services only. It seems that the Diocese was desperately short of substitute clergy in its far western reaches.

Patrick used the master's degree I'd encouraged him to earn summers while I taught in Thornton to land a post on a junior college faculty in Stark, Illinois teaching Latin and Comparative Religions until he was old enough to retire.

CHAPTER TWO

The Book and Place to Resolve the Problem

Disabled moving van

What does a librarian do when she is faced with a problem? She consults a book on the subject. In studying how best to provide on a recently divorced librarian's salary with four offspring, I ran across this incredibly appropriate book entitled <u>One Acre and Security</u>. The male author gives sensible advice about raising your own food via a large garden and small livestock such as rabbits, chickens, and bees…all upon a single acre.

Since I had just closed out my public-school teachers' retirement upon acquiring tenure on the River City College faculty, that tidy sum could serve as a down payment upon a house and the one acre specified for SECURITY! My offspring ranged from enthusiastic to ambivalent.

Susan, my oldest, was about to leave for her freshman year at the University of Illinois double majoring in Performance Piano and Nursing, so whatever I wanted to do was OK by her. She could inspect and enjoy the results on her breaks and vacations.

Ron, the only boy and second of my first pair, liked apartment life near urban amenities, so he was not too enthusiastic as I described the small country estate I hoped to purchase for our family. (He had friends who had yard work and snow removal duties that didn't sound like much fun) He was attending Kent Country Day School courtesy of his doctor father and transporting him the 90 miles each way from Swerlin had added much to my parenting duties prior to the divorce.

Martha, still in grade school and going to be bused to an alternative Gifted Program across town, was genuinely enthusiastic about moving to a place where we could have lots of animals. We could only have one cat in the apartment.

Patty, the youngest and only child by my second husband and thanks to a hotly contested divorce, visited every weekend from Swerlin. Her father and I alternated driving her the 90 miles between our homes on Friday evenings and returning her late on Sundays. So much for the divorce ending the strenuous commuting.

After living in the vicarage under supervision of the Bishop's

Committee, I longed to once again own my own home. With Susan safely deposited at the University of Illinois and Patty visiting every weekend, Ron, Martha and I settled into life at the apartment complex. Each had a bedroom (which meant Patty shared Martha's on weekends), we had the most necessary furniture and were gradually augmenting that from garage sales and trips to the Salvation and Good Will stores. The grocery store was just a short walk away, and there were lots of other young people around.

Martha made friends easily, but Ron mainly depended upon Kent School contacts during weekdays. We were careful to attend most extracurricular events for both youngsters...basketball games in which Ron played and the P.T.O. Carnival and holiday programs for Martha. She also asked to take gymnastic lessons, and recalling her disappointment at not being permitted to play Little League in Swerlin, I quickly assented to that and guitar lessons. There were so many opportunities in River City that had not been available in Swerlin.

We joined a small Episcopal Church where they desperately drafted me to replace their departing organist. Ron had volunteered me at the coffee hour following the Sunday service we attended there. I had to draw the priest aside to explain our divorced situation before giving an affirmative answer. Divorce among the Episcopalian clergy was a great scandal then and I was fearful that I might be excommunicated or at least not permitted to take Holy Communion.

The priest reassured me that we were all most welcome to attend this small mission church nor would we be considered second-class Christians. What a relief to be permitted to take Holy Communion, but what a strain to have to play their old push pedal organ each Sunday! I would practice diligently and then take two tranquilizers to keep my hands from shaking on the keys. Since most of the hymns were familiar, I managed...finding new mistakes to make occasionally. St. Stephen's could not afford to pay their organist, and I was worth every bit of that salary. What a gift from God when a real organist appeared on the scene and I only played as "relief" occasionally.

The children attended Christian education classes, and few people knew that Patty did not live with me full-time. I figured it was none of their business that I drove out Friday nights…three hours round-trip to pick her up and another three hours on late Sunday afternoons to return her. Since Patrick and I alternated these driving chores, I only had to do that every other weekend. It was an improvement over driving that route five days a week as I had when I first began working at River City College so that Ron could attend private school and escape the bullying he'd endured in Swerlin public schools. So much of life is…compared to whatever.

Life was proceeding relatively smoothly until Susan came home one fall weekend to attend a wedding shower for one of her Swerlin classmates. She borrowed the car for that afternoon and evening. Well past the time she should have been home the phone rang.

Susan's mitten had slid off the front seat on her way home and when she leaned over to retrieve it, she let one of the front wheels run off the pavement. In attempting to get back on the pavement, she lost control. My car had careened across the road, rolled over, and slid on one side down an embankment. This information was related by Susan's classmate's father who had retrieved Susan from the Emergency Room at Swerlin Hospital, bruised but not seriously hurt.

I, of course, was first of all immensely grateful that Susan had not been badly hurt. The next concern was the state of our one-and-only car. It had been towed to the Standard gas station in Swerlin, and the owner thought it might be fixable. Anyway, Susan would stay the night with her classmate whose father would bring her to River City in time to catch her ride back to Illinois University.

Fortunately, the car was declared "totaled" by the insurance adjuster and no, they would make no allowance for the new set of tires I had just put on the vehicle for expected winter driving. Now I would have to add car payments to my other financial obligations.

The Volkswagen dealer offered me an irresistible deal on a "Thing", a German jeep-like vehicle manufactured in Mexico. Ron enjoyed pulling out the isinglass side window on the passenger side and tossing it into the back seat before climbing in, this in front of his admiring Kent classmates who, poor deprived kids, were awaiting their prosaic rides in Lincolns or Cadillacs.

A very annoying attribute of the Thing was that its gas heater warmed up at the beginning of one's ride and then cut off for the remainder of the trip. Consequently, I took to wearing an old fur jacket and pulling a blanket throw over my knees when going very far. One Sunday evening, while returning to River City after delivering Patty back to Swerlin, I was pulled over by a policeman.

"Do you realize you were doing 70 miles per hour when the speed limit along here is posted as 60?" he asked.

"Oh my...I didn't know this Thing could go that fast," I exclaimed.

He saw how bundled up I was and let me off with a warning. 'Another time God rescued me from impending trouble.

It was December 1976 shortly before Christmas when the lump sum settlement from my secondary school teachers' retirement arrived. Ever since I'd been granted tenure on the River City College faculty the previous spring we'd been looking around for a home of our own for which the pension money could be used as a down payment. After ten years in a vicarage, subject to the whims and budget of the church's governing board, I desperately wanted our very own place.

Although $8,000 seemed a vast amount to our family who lived on a meager librarian's salary plus $150 per month ($50 per child to guarantee their doctor father's visiting rights), it meant finding a modest home in the $30,000 range. Few of such properties had much in the way of grounds around them, and how could we grow much of our own food unless we had room for a garden, fruit trees, and berry bushes, to say nothing about housing for rabbits and chickens, etc. If we could only find a three- bedroom house with a large garage and about an acre of land!

We drove all over the River City area attending open houses on Sunday afternoons. Martha could be bused to her gifted program from anywhere in the River City School System, and I transported Ron to and from private school, so we had quite a large area to scan for a suitable place.

The week before Christmas our realtor called about an interesting place just listed. It was a small club house on a bankrupt golf course off Norburg Road almost to the next county line. We piled into the car to go see and were enchanted by the unique building. It was completely uninsulated, so quite frigid, but occupied by the owner's son who used it as an artist's studio. It had a huge central area with a loft circling the second floor as the veranda outside circled the first floor. An exposed partial basement on the lower side was used as a garage and storage area.

The club house had been split off from the rest of the defunct golf course, so it had about half an acre of grounds and a very steep, rough driveway up to the road. The kids each wanted a portion of the loft for bedrooms, and I lusted after the space and chance to decorate it into something special HOUSE AND GARDEN magazine might want to feature.

A couple of newlyweds were also touring the property when we arrived. I had my realtor immediately place a bid at the asking price—a bit beyond my means. The day before Christmas she called back with word that the newlyweds had been able to gain their families' backing for a bid $5,000 over the asking price. I had to capitulate. The kids were very disappointed as well, and I asked God later that night some questions about "the time wasted and dashed hopes close to a holiday." We'd even driven Susan out to show her what we'd bid for.

Two days after Christmas my ever-optimistic realtor called again. She genuinely felt sorry about the aborted transaction and not just because of her missed commission. She had a listing that might interest us—nearly an acre with fruit trees, but the house only had two bedrooms. We agreed to look at it. The owner wanted to retire to a real farm and was anxious to find a buyer, anxious enough to accept a bid lower than the asking price she assured me.

The kids have since kidded me that I fell in love with the fireplace and huge trees. It had both a fenced in front and back yard so we could finally have a dog. A giant blue spruce tree dominated the back yard while twin firs marked the corners of the front yard with huge maples shading the front of the house. There were only two bedrooms and one bathroom in the original house, but a knotty-pine family room had been added to the entire length of the back with a giant fireplace. The kitchen overlooked it and was connected by the landing to the basement stairs and three steps up to it. I could join in on the conversation or watch television while preparing meals. The former attached garage was an unheated, glassed-in summer porch which formed an air lock winter entrance to the family room.

A full basement to the original house had a large carpeted room plus a shower and sink beside the furnace, hot water heater, water softener, and wall of shelves. Small windows let in some light, and my son agreed he'd like the "basement apartment". That solved the two-bedroom dilemma, but the only full bathroom was entered through the smaller bedroom...a feature which had kept this otherwise nifty home from selling. (I decided to place a curtain divider to form a narrow hallway through to the bathroom, but I kept that solution to myself.)

The newer two-car detached garage with a workshop behind the car stalls (heated by a wood burning stove) was the final selling point. The remains of a huge garden beyond the backyard fence made my source book <u>One Acre and Security</u> seem viable.

My first offer was rejected, but a second one slightly higher was accepted. We rejoiced and kept driving by daily with very proprietary looks while mortgage and closing arrangements were made. As a neophyte buyer, I was caught short by the closing costs. I called my former doctor husband and he agreed to forward one year's child support in advance to help me out, so the first year in our new home proved to be a financially strapped one. However, we had a home of our own again finally.

The former owners agreed to leave curtains, stove, and refrigerator in place for us apartment dwellers. I hired a U-Haul truck to transport the rest of our belongings across town. When I reported to pick it up, they only had a larger truck than originally agreed upon, but said they would give it to me for the same price as the smaller one. Probably one trip would do it with this larger truck, so I lurched out gingerly and managed to back the truck to the curb near the patio doors in our first-floor apartment.

We started loading about eleven o'clock a.m. Saturday and we (Ron, Martha, Patty and I) had wrestled everything aboard the truck by four p.m. Patty joined me in the truck's cab, holding our cat, and the other children rode with my elderly retired school librarian friend, Mildred Kilely, who had offered to pick up fried chicken dinners for our first meal in our new home.

We carefully negotiated traffic the ten miles across River City and turned into our small, dead end 16th Street. The entrance to our long driveway half way down the blacktopped road was marked by a pair of wagon wheels anchored by large concrete bases. As I turned into the driveway, the left rear wheel of the large rental truck upended the wagon wheel base under the rear of the truck. I could neither go forward nor backward, and the cab was raised onto a slant, too.

Our new neighbors came out to view this interesting development while Patty with the cat and I climbed very carefully out of the upper side of the cab. Now Saturday evening is not an opportune time to find a tow truck, and several refused to tackle my situation as I described it over the phone. At last a tow truck operator agreed to come and see if he could get the truck down off the wheel, but it would be at least an hour before he could break away from other things underway.

Miss Kiley wished me luck, but because she didn't like to drive after dark, she drove away with the only workable wheels. We sat cross-legged in the carpeted kitchen to eat our chicken dinners. Since we had all missed lunch in the throes of loading the truck, that chicken was especially delicious. We gave great thanks as we prayed grace over it and for the tow truck man coming to help us gain access to our beds and other belongings.

Then Patty's father arrived, angry and upset about the move, to pick up Patty and transport her back to Swerlin from our new location. I'd left a note and map since I couldn't reach him by phone. He didn't offer any assistance with the upended truck, just gave me a piece of his angry mind and departed with his darling daughter.

The last of the neighbors had disappeared and daylight was fading when the tow truck driver and his skeptical buddy arrived at last. They roared with laughter and said they'd never seen such a funny predicament.

"Only a woman driver could have gotten herself into such a fix!"

We were dead tired and desperate, but laughed along with them while they looked over the degree of land slope and truck slope plus the shape of the wagon wheel base. They decided to pull the truck straight on forward and beyond the wagon wheel...then tow the wagon wheel and its base back into place. It took them less than ten minutes, the truck was slightly scratched underneath, and I had AAA towing insurance to reimburse the costs. We gave hearty thanks to our rescuers.

Then we unloaded and set up our beds, collapsed into them, and left the rest of the unpacking until morning. We were on our own property, in our own house, with the prospect of independence and security ahead.

CHAPTER THREE

Our Livestock and Garden

Watch out for angry bees

As for livestock, our guiding book <u>One Acre and Security</u> recommended raising rabbits and chickens for meat. We thought rabbits would be nice, but none of us was about to kill or cook a gentle bunny. Maybe we could have some angora rabbits whose coats we could shear and sell to bring in money for meat. Chickens would annoy the neighbors, so they were ruled out. But bees were a possibility.

The Sears Farm and Suburban Catalog advertised bees and everything needed to get started with them—hives to assemble, wax trays for honey foundations, gloves and netted helmet to protect oneself while tending, smokers to quiet bees, a hive tool to pry hive sections apart, etc.

I was enchanted, remembering from my girlhood how I'd watched my mother's best friend, Marie, tend bees in her prolific backyard garden. Of course, Marie was an Italian immigrant with no children or job outside her home. That garden and keeping her home spotless and supplied with home-cooked goodies for husband Ernest were her main occupations. I'd sit by the summer hour on her shaded back steps and visit with Marie while she weeded, watered, and picked her many small crops. But the most fascinating of Marie's activities was tending her bees. She never put on protective clothing, but was sure to wear light colored shorts and top around the hives. Nor was she afraid of the bees, so they were used to her scent and there was mutual acceptance.

Marie was careful to leave the bees plenty of their own honey to sustain them over the winter. She also kept a filter layer so the larger queen bee remained toward the bottom of the hive while the smaller worker bees could reach and fill an extra super layer for Marie's uses…honey and her own beeswax candles which she used for home and gifts.

Early the next spring (after the child support payments were resumed) I ordered one of the hives-to-be-assembled plus the smoker, veiled helmet, and hive prying tool. Since I am not very handy with tools, the assembling took quite a while in and around other demands on my time. Part by part the hive was completed and painted white. The project was housed in the former attached garage which had been converted into an unheated summer porch with windows all along the yard side, shaded by an immense maple tree which surely predated the house.

Several weeks later all was ready for the bees to inhabit the single hive out in the shade of the giant lilac bushes in the farthest corner of the fenced-in back yard. I ordered the bees and waited impatiently, now that my own drawn out preparations had been accomplished. Then one Sunday afternoon, as I climbed out of my Volkswagen Beetle following the church picnic, my son rushed out to tell me that the Sears people had been calling me frantically several times over the past two hours to come and get my bees immediately. Since bees are live items, I assumed the clerks were anxious to deliver their bees in healthy condition, so I phoned to assure them I'd be there to pick up the bees in half an hour. "Hurry!" the voice on the phone pleaded.

The reason I was to hurry turned out to be a stray bee picked up in transit who was crawling on the outside of the container… probably attracted by the queen bee's scent. She is shipped in a small cage within the container of hundreds of worker bees. I signed for my buzzing package and headed for the closest exit, the bonus bee hanging tightly to the moving box. Although I left all the car windows open on the way home, that bee was not enticed away.

Enclosed with the package were elaborate instructions about how to release the bees into the hive and where to place the sugar-coated queen's cage so the worker bees could eat through it and let her out. I donned my bee paraphernalia, opened the hive, and gently shook the bees into it. Then I placed the queen's cage properly, closed the hive, and made sure there was an ample supply of sugar-water nearby to assist the bees in their initial period of adjustment.

These bees were quite large, Italian bees advertised to be of a gentle variety. After all, this was my first hive and I needed all the help I could get. Veteran beekeepers advised starting with two hives, but I couldn't afford a second hive. Things seemed to go well with the bees. 'Ideal livestock, we could leave for a two-week vacation in August and they'd care for themselves while we were gone. I decided against taking any honey for ourselves that first year, for the bees might need all they had produced for themselves.

As winter approached, I became very concerned about how cold our Indiana winters would seem to Italian bees. Then because I could not afford to lose my single hive, I decided to move it indoors on the unheated summer porch to minimize wind, snow, and sleet damage to the hive and its humming occupants. One November night I smoked the hive, blocked its main entrance, and wheeled the hive onto the back porch using a borrowed refrigerator dolly.

No, none of my beekeeper's guides suggested this sort of wintering; it was my very own strategy. Occasionally on sunny winter days I'd find an adventurous bee plastered to a cold window pane. One March day there were so many bees circulating on the porch that I thought the time had come to borrow the refrigerator dolly and transport the hive outdoors again—down the long back sidewalk to its original location near the lilac bushes.

None of the kids wished to help. After all, they explained, I had only one veiled helmet, so they'd watch from the family room windows. In broad daylight I propped the porch door open, slid the dolly under the hive, eased down the one low step from the porch, and began a rapid roll down the sidewalk. Unfortunately, the winter weather had heaved one section of the sidewalk and as I hit that place going a fair clip, the dolly tipped and the top layer of the hive and its cover went sideways with a crash.

Since the bees regarded this as distinctly hostile behavior, I went for a world record scrambling back to the house, the bees in hot pursuit. Several caught up with and wounded me while others beat me to the house and through the door my son thoughtfully held open.

What could I do now? The hive was in the middle of the backyard, its top section and cover off, and the short March daylight was beginning to fade. In addition, I had to retrieve the refrigerator dolly to return that night besides getting the hive back to where it belonged with its top section and lid on properly. I didn't want to lose those bees after their making it through the winter. Well, more from desperation than courage, I put on my heaviest winter outerwear plus my beekeeper's protective gear. The kids tossed for who would hold open the back door this time, and Ron lost.

Then I tiptoed out the front door and down the far side of the house. Quickly I peered around the corner to plot my fewest moves to accomplish my objectives. The main part of the hive was still on the dolly pointed in the right direction. Should I just continue with it and come back for the separated top and hive cover? Probably not—I had a suspicion that I'd only get a single pass for this mercy run, so I'd better reassemble the hive quickly, push the whole thing to its intended place, disengage the dolly, and roar back to the house with the dolly in tow. As before, the kids were watching with great interest. They'd wished me good luck and I'd brushed that aside with, "Never mind wishing, PRAY...and be ready to open that back door!"

The top and the lid may not have been perfectly aligned, but I wasn't seeking perfection that evening, just survival for the bees and me. Miraculously for once, things went according to plan. While several bees were brushed off my clothing later, I had no additional stings. Never again, however, did I attempt to winter bees inside.

A second hive added the second year raised my hopes for honey. However, an allergic neighbor threatened to sue me, so we sold out to a local beekeeper at a loss and settled for pets instead of the recommended livestock. Besides, Aldi's had added frozen food to their stock of cheap groceries and I knew dozens of ways to fix hamburger.

Our vegetable garden was a good idea and did produce lovely fresh lettuce, radishes, cabbages, squash, and carrots—all from cheap seed. Noting the cost of tomato starts, however, I started my own from seed in pared down milk cartons filled with potting soil. Proudly I set out sixty of the resulting small plants which the rabbits or other wild things consumed that same night. After weeks of watering and tending them, my tomato starts were wiped out.

The other garden aspect was that we always attended the two-week family reunion the first two weeks of August back in the cabin my father built on a table-top mountain in western Pennsylvania. This was exactly harvest time for freezing or canning one's garden surplus. By the time we returned to Indiana from Pennsylvania our garden was a tangle of giant weeds, its surplus rotting or consumed by birds and wild animals.

Two continuing successes in our projected food production were the raspberry bushes planted by the previous owner along the side fence back of the garage and the apples from the inherited apple tree. The rugged raspberry bushes continued to produce good sized, flavorful berries from early summer to mid-September. I learned to destroy the tent caterpillars when they invaded our apple tree by waiting until the wee critters returned home to their tent at evening and then setting their tent on fire.

Since the apple harvest came after we had returned from vacation, I was able to put up applesauce and make a few apple pies besides eating our fill of them with lunches and as snacks.

Because I believed children should have pets to train and be responsible for, we had a large tomcat named Harvey and having a fenced-in backyard at our Retreat, we adopted a small dog from the Pound. We named our mutt of many breeds, so ugly he was cute, "Rascal."

Harvey was a typical gray and black striped tomcat who would disappear for weeks at a time on what we assumed were excursions to romance felines far and near. There did seem to be a profusion of young tiger-striped kittens in the area. Often Harvey would reappear bloodied and exhausted...home to recuperate before his next foray. After five years of such goings and returnings, one winter day I found his frozen carcass behind the workshop. He'd managed to make it home to die.

Rascal also had a yen to wander. Whenever the backyard gate

was not secured properly, our dog would paw open the gate, give us a doggy grin if we called him to come back, and keep on going. Meal times brought him home, barking to be forgiven and welcomed back. I was down to one teenager and the dog when one of Rascal's escapes went on permanently. He simply disappeared.

Ron noted when we got settled in our new home that the side lawn was "as big as a football field"!

"Our football field," I enthused. "If you mow that, I'll mow the front and back yards." He took on the mowing task, but he often complained. Somehow, despite all the good advice in our <u>One Acre and Security</u> text, we never became securely self-sufficient.

CHAPTER FOUR

Son Ron and Private School

I had originally ordered six boys from the Lord, life being so complex and not straight forward for girls. Since we humans have very little to say about such matters, I received instead three daughters and one son. Ronell Scott arrived six months prematurely as the doctor's and my second child. Ron was named after his paternal grandfather, a professor of soil physics in the Agronomy Department at Indiana. Since I had lived with Morgan's parents during the two upper classman years at the U. of Indiana, I also loved his father. We'd attended football games together and talked and laughed about many things as we commuted daily from their country home to the Unity campus while Morgan was off in Cranston at Medical School.

Both our older children were born at the Army's expense. Because there was a shortage of government housing in Germany, Morgan's overseas assignment after basic training, he rented space in a castle so baby Susan and I could join him in Arbach, northern Bavaria. Living in three rooms of the twenty-eight-room castle, a huge gray stone edifice twelve kilometers from Arbach, was quite an experience.

Baron Von Shal, the owner, had been a prisoner of war in the United States during the latter part of World War II. His English was quite good, but he was the only person in the castle or its village who did speak English. The only telephone was in the village's small saloon called a gasthaus. During World War II this castle became a rest and rehabilitation center for Allied officers who had rifled the wine cellar. Now the Baron raised catfish commercially in the moat.

No longer could the drawbridge be raised; it just provided a grand entrance.

The castle was presided over by the Baron's widowed mother who couldn't fathom why my advanced education had not included French, the international language in her hey-day. My baby Susan delighted the elderly Baroness since her son still hadn't married to provide her with any grandchildren.

Sometime later. after moving into government quarters in Arbach and teaching a year of kindergarten for American dependents, Ron was born in the Army hospital in Munich. I'd been ferried there from our base in Arbach because of premature labor pains. The doctor placed me on total bed rest and medications to prolong the pregnancy and give the baby a better chance. A long week passed during which I read the three volumes of the Civil War trilogy <u>Lee's Lieutenants</u> by Douglas Freeman. (My husband was a Civil War buff, so that's what he provided when I begged for something to read to help pass the off-my-feet time. It also explains why our oldest girl's middle name is "Lee" after the gallant Southern general.) Anyway, on the sixth night before the day I was to go home since I'd been painless for two days, the labor pains returned more savage than before. The staff repeated their previous moves to offset delivery, but the birth was not to be deterred this time. Just ahead of two a.m. a very tiny and fragile Ron was born and rushed into a "preemie" incubator.

His father had been roused from sleep, first to report serious labor pains and later to report that he had a newborn son. I struggled against exhaustion to await Morgan's arrival, and when enough time for a round trip had elapsed, asked the nurse to call him again. "Oh, I'll see them in the morning," was the unimpressed medical spouse's reply. Having somehow expected more, I cried myself to sleep. True to his word, Morgan arrived about ten a.m. with a dozen yellow (his favorite color) roses.

Because Ron was a preemie, I was not permitted to attend to him in a portable bassinet in my room as the other new mothers did their offspring. I had to return home empty-armed, having only seen my son through the glass of the nursery window and the additional glass of his incubator. I called twice a day to check on Ron' weight and condition. Every other day and then daily I journeyed to the hospital to yearn through the nursery window over his tiny frame as he continued to lose weight one ounce at a time.

Finally, a male medical corpsman made Ron a private project, coming in around the clock every three hours to hold and tickle our sleepy son into taking his formula and wanting to live. The weight stabilized and then Ron began to gain slowly. I finally got to cuddle and take him home at five pounds when he was six weeks old.

Ron had to be kept in a back bedroom and isolated from his sister Susan (eighteen months older) who might carry disease germs or upset his strict eating and sleeping regimen. Understandably, Susan resented the little newcomer who required so much of her mommy's time and attention.

Not being allowed to see and touch her baby brother, she developed a jealous dislike of him. Always a gal of action, I caught her in Ron's room trying to hit him in the head with her daddy's hammer. She only got in a glancing blow, but Morgan was afraid his son might be mentally challenged from that or the two times Ron ran such high fevers that first year when I soaked him in tepid water containing rubbing alcohol to bring down the high fever and arrest the jerky motions just short of seizures.

Morgan always regarded any family infirmity as a personal affront—his German and medical background, I guess. Anyway, he was very busy supervising the base's medical facility and away a lot, so the children's care rested mainly upon me and a full-time German housemaid.

Liza was a gift at that point, somehow passed on by the apartment's previous tenant. Her quarters were in the basement of the apartment building along with those of the other maids. She took young Susan in hand and, as I learned later, passed her off as Liza's own while shopping in the marketplace. Each day Liza would tuck Susan into an elaborate German stroller with large chrome fenders and a small featherbed during cold snaps, and fill a string bag on the handlebars with the fresh German produce which Americans were warned against eating. Since both Morgan and I had suffered microbe acclimation dubbed "Hitler's Revenge" soon after arriving in Germany, we ignored the warning and ate very well for less than our Commissary shopping friends.

Susan learned to speak German with Liza and English with us, never confusing the two languages. I got to gradually enlarge baby Ron's surroundings and stimulate his taste for life after such a traumatic beginning. He grew plump and healthier, but was a timid and late walker and later talker. Susan had finally accepted him as her little (and lower) brother, so she kept interpreting for him in her quick, bright way. He had little reason to learn to talk, and he continued to be in Susan's shadow through early years of schooling.

When we had returned to this country, our mandatory two years of military service for all doctors completed, Morgan took over an abandoned family practice in Patton, Illinois about twenty-five miles north of Unity. We lived in a bungalow the town had constructed for a native World War II veteran's return from service but who now inhabited a larger home as his family had increased in size.

I became Morgan's office assistant with Ron in a playpen next to my receptionist desk the first year. Slowly the practice grew and deadbeats from every direction found us. I was torn between ministering to patients on the phone and in the office on top of caring for my young son. Things came to a head when I had to bring Ron to the office despite his running a fever. I demanded I be allowed to get a teaching job from which I could take time off with a sick child plus get paid to spend vacations and holidays with our two children. Morgan was earning enough now to hire a nurse/receptionist, so he benefited from having someone with medical training as his assistant.

After three years of being a general practitioner, Morgan decided he'd like to take advanced training to become a specialist in a single medical field. He found it impossible to keep up with all the fields involved with a general family practice. For six months we reviewed together all kinds of specialties except surgery. He knew his future didn't include his becoming a surgeon.

At last Morgan settled on anesthesiology, a field narrow enough he could master it completely. The closest training program was offered in Charleston, Illinois. I suggested he immediately apply for entrance which he did, but believed he was too late in June for the next class starting in September. Wrong! His immediate acceptance gave us only two months to close the family practice, sell the bungalow, find housing in Illinois plus a teaching job for me.

God was so good! A rental home occupied by a finishing medical student's family became available in Raceway next door to Charleston. With that street address I was hired to teach English in a huge consolidated high school nearby. A grandmotherly woman down the block from our new home agreed to become our babysitter for a reasonable salary.

Morgan announced the closing of his practice, sent final bills, and listed our Illinois address to mail what was still due. Only about half was paid off during the next two years, but each amount was gratefully received.

I enjoyed teaching which included two gifted English classes. When I inquired why the newest English teacher was given such a pleasurable assignment as teaching gifted students, I was told no one else wanted these classes because those students asked too many questions. To balance the gifted classes, I was also assigned two slow classes filled with students waiting to flunk out or to quit school on their sixteenth birthdays and get jobs.

The gifted classes completed their usual ninth grade curriculum by Christmas and spent the spring semester writing research papers on topics of their own mentored choice and sharing aloud the results with their fellow students. My slow classes learned very practical language skills like writing letters, filling out job applications, composing resumes, etc.

I also became faculty advisor to the yearbook staff. I was a real neophyte at that, but the student staff was primarily composed of juniors and seniors who had already turned out several yearbooks. Together we produced that year's book with especially creative division pages. In a yearbook competition that yearbook won for me, its advisor, a summer course at the School of Journalism at the University of Indiana. The prize was announced in Indianapolis newspapers which didn't please Morgan who always expected to be the center of attention.

My second year at the high school besides teaching I was drafted to be the debate squad's coach while their usual advisor took a year's sabbatical to complete a graduate degree. Since I had been a member of the University of Indiana's Varsity Debate Squad (the only woman and only member not in pre-law) I was a natural choice. However, traveling to tournaments on Saturdays in their very long season (September to May) increased both babysitting and transportation costs.

Morgan was nearing the end of his training in anesthesiology and had already obtained the promise of a position with Caring Clinic in his Indiana hometown. I was looking forward to finally becoming a full-time homemaker and mother. It seemed high time to have another child, so I suspended my birth control method and learned I was pregnant with our third child in April.

When Morgan called to say he'd be home for supper the next evening, I fixed an especially elaborate meal in honor of sharing the news about our coming baby. Once the two kids were through their bedtime rituals and asleep, I sat down happily to talk with Morgan. Before I managed to relate my good news, Morgan told me that he wanted a divorce. It seems that a beautiful nurse had convinced him that I didn't have enough social graces to be the wife of a specialist. Why, I didn't even play golf! She had been a beauty queen before nursing studies and her folks had been society leaders back in Potstown, Illinois.

I sat stunned and disbelieving. Then I blurted out, "You can't have a divorce after all we've been through to get you qualified and now we're expecting our third child!"

"You didn't ask my permission," he retorted. "You'd better get an abortion quickly. I don't want to pay child support for more than the two we already have."

"Abortion? That's illegal and immoral…and you a doctor dare suggest that?"

"We both know abortions are readily available," he countered as I began to cry. "Well, I'd better get back to the hospital. We'll discuss future arrangements some other time," and Morgan left.

I delayed, hoping our marriage could be saved. Future arrangements included telling his folks during a previously booked weekend visit. They, of course, were flabbergasted. After leaving his parents' home, we stopped in a local park because an argument had become so heated. I jumped out of the car and started walking. Suddenly I heard the car start up behind me and looking back, I saw a wild-eyed Morgan at the wheel speeding right toward me. I jumped behind the nearest tree so he missed running me over.

The kids in the back seat (no child seats in that day) shouted and cried which brought Morgan to his senses. He turned the car around and came slowly back to me. I returned to the passenger seat and told him,"If you want a divorce that badly, you can have it, but somebody has to raise our kids!" Then reassuring Susan and Ron, we rode silently on toward Indiana.

Eventually, with the help of a psychiatrist recommended by my priest, I accepted that it takes two to make a successful marriage and there was no way I could save our marriage by myself. Then Morgan and I worked out divorce terms. I would have the children and a house. Alimony would only last two years while I completed a graduate degree to qualify for better jobs and make up for the graduate assistantship I had surrendered to marry Morgan. Contrary to advice from my lawyer and parents, I only requested fifty dollars per child per month—the minimum required by Illinois law to guarantee Morgan's visiting privileges. He would see his children at

Thanksgiving for an early Christmas and two weeks each summer for a vacation.

Morgan's folks helped him obtain a small home on Rainbow View in Unity for me and the kids. (Our house was one block ahead of Easy Street, the story of my life, I thought.) Morgan took an apartment in August when we all moved back to Indiana. Since one needs to have lived in Indiana for a year before obtaining a divorce, Martha was born while we were still married.

My Caring Clinic obstetrician asked if I would like him to call Morgan to be present at my baby's birth, but I responded. "No, he never made the birth of any of our other children." A bouquet of yellow roses did arrive the day after.

Martha's birth began another sad period in young Ron's life. He developed an inability to walk and had to be carried everywhere. After extensive testing, this was deemed to be psychosomatic—an unintentional reaction to having to compete with the new baby for his mother's attention. I took off a semester from Library School classes to spend additional time with Ron, keeping wee Martha in a far corner of my bedroom and away from his usual activities. The strategy brought Ron back his mobility, but I was made aware of how much my son missed his father and really needed one. That was a factor in my accepting the offer of marriage from Rev. Patrick plus I doubted a woman with three young children would receive many proposals.

Unfortunately, Patrick and Ron did not get along well much of the time we lived in Swerlin. On top of that, Ron grew slowly so he was smaller than most of his male classmates in that tough river town where wrestling was the major sport. Nor did we own a boat or indulge in water sports like many of his classmates' families.

When not in school or delivering newspapers, Ron spent most of his time in his room avoiding his priestly stepfather. Then Ron had to be enrolled in a private school because the bullying at public school had become too much. This solution was instigated by a psychiatrist hired by Morgan (on the kids' vacation with him) to discover what was wrong with his only son.

Ron did prosper at Kent Country Day School in River City, Illinois that he entered in the eighth grade and continued until high school graduation. For two years he and I commuted the ninety miles each way on weekdays. It was a grueling arrangement—working as Public Services Librarian and Archivist at River City College from 8:30 a.m. to 4:30 p.m., picking Ron up at school and heading home for a late supper. Then we would rise at 5:00 a.m. for breakfast and repeat the same ninety miles again.

As a sophomore, Ron had a chance to play varsity basketball since he had grown taller and filled out physically. Having been raised with three sisters, I believed time on a male team would greatly benefit him. We secured an apartment in River City so he could make after-school practices and Friday night games, only returning to Swerlin early Saturday morning for weekends.

Susan was old enough to prepare simple meals I planned and shopped for with Martha's help, but weekends were hectic with housecleaning, laundry and church duties. Besides, I was coming up for consideration as a tenured member of the permanent faculty, so I needed a River City area address.

My marriage to Fr. Patrick was faltering, but Susan, my oldest, was scheduled to graduate as valedictorian of her high school class and I hung on rather than rob her of this honor. Once she graduated, however, I gradually moved most of the rest of Ron's and my belongings to the River City apartment even though Fr. Patrick didn't even notice.

Our family had survived three separate attempts by disgruntled parishioners to have Patrick removed as Vicar of St. James, but things had settled down. He called on parishioners on Wednesday afternoons. They often arranged not to be home, but he always left a calling card so they would know he'd done his duty. His long, erudite sermons frequently displaying his knowledge of Greek and Latin derivations continued. He was meticulous about getting his reports in to the Diocese of Cranston on time. He attended Rotary meetings, listened to Cranston Cubs games, and read a great deal. He did expect meals on time and even taught Ron to say Grace before meals in Latin which Ron can still recite.

Fr. Patrick did have one chance to interview for a pastorate in a town just thirty miles south of River City. I hoped this would be successful and perhaps save our marriage, but during Patrick's and my interview visit Patrick pointed out to their search committee all the repairs and renovations needed to their church and its rectory. He considered himself a building expert, but that was not the type of priest they were looking for and they failed to elect him.

After that misfortune I consulted a lawyer about getting a divorce. The lawyer advised that Patrick and I come to terms before going to court, but this proved to be impossible. Patrick was adamant that he retain custody of his daughter Patty. He even got an injunction making me return her to Swerlin and then delayed further proceedings until after school started in September. The judge then ruled that I retain custody of the three Stauffer children and Patrick have Patty with the proviso that she spend every weekend with me in River City, Patrick and I driving both ways on alternate weekends. So much for the divorce being the end of my commuting!

Freed of contact with his resented stepfather and the bullying he had suffered in Swerlin schools, Ron prospered in private school, then entered River City College tuition-free because I was on the faculty. He chose a pre-med program, and Morgan agreed to fund Ron's living expenses in an all-male dormitory.

Ron entered his new environment with much enthusiasm. Since he had been able to master his high school studies without much effort, he assumed the same would hold true for college courses. 'Not with pre-med, it turned out. Ron flunked out of his freshman year having spent a great deal of his time as a disk jockey on the college's radio station and playing ongoing games of "Dragons & Dungeons" in his dorm's lounge.

Naturally I was embarrassed, but quickly got him back home

and enrolled in our local junior college where he redeemed himself. With that improved record, Ron qualified to transfer to Northern Indiana University in Dorian. I was breathing easier about Ron's finally getting a four-year degree when he flunked "Statistics" his senior year and would have to repeat the course before he could graduate.

His doctor father protested that he had funded enough education for Ron—private school from eighth grade through high school, dorm living for one year at River City College and two years at Northern Indiana University. Ron would have to pay his own way now. Ron retaliated and surprised all of us by joining the Air Force.

Military discipline proved beneficial and Ron completed his Bachelor's Degree online at a small college while in the Service. He intended to make a career of the military, but roused some ire among higher officers with a letter to the base newspaper suggesting some improvements to the Air Force. When he took the examination he needed to pass to qualify for the next grade or be retired, the pass score was drawn one point above what he had scored and Ron was mustered out just months ahead of the ten years required for a pension.

Returning to River City, Ron got a job with a manufacturer of machine parts using his computer skills to manage their giant warehouse from which parts are shipped all over the world. Ron had finally blossomed and was competing successfully in the larger world.

CHAPTER FIVE

The Would-be Nun and Us

Elizabeth Samuelson attended our church and Sunday School, so we knew her well as a contemporary of my oldest daughter Susan. Although she was not pretty, she had long black hair…halfway down her back…brown eyes, a fair complexion, and a pleasant expression with a ready smile. Unfortunately, a pronounced limp remained from a childhood injury which kept Beth from participating in sports and made her very self-conscious.

Although her appearance was slightly marred, there was nothing wrong with Beth's intelligence and superb memory. She had a brother ten years her senior who was the apple of her parents' eyes. While she didn't lack encouragement, Beth was a lonely child growing up, an after-thought of older parents.

Since she gravitated on Sundays toward me and my active crew, we often included her on our local excursions. I congratulated her on her straight-A report cards and encouraged her to attend college. When she reported that her parents had no such plans because such an expense would compromise their retirement funds, I offered to check into scholarship possibilities at River City College.

Partial scholarships were readily available for such a capable scholar, but Beth would need a full scholarship. We decided to pray about a way for her to go to college and enlisted prayer support from the entire congregation. In answer, one of our male church members who was very active in the local Rotary organization recommended Beth for a two-year scholarship (tuition and textbooks) to the junior college if she could continue living at home. Her parents consented but indicated that after she graduated, she would be on her own.

This was less than I'd hoped for, but counseled Beth that her junior college credits could be transferred toward a four-year degree. It was surely an answer to prayer and a positive step in the direction of her dreams.

I attended Beth's high school graduation and met her parents plus her older brother, a successful car salesman with a wife and infant son. They were proud of Beth's being on the Honor Roll and among the top ten graduates. During the reception following the ceremony, Beth's father pulled me aside and thanked me for encouraging Beth, but he cautioned me that junior college was the end of their support. It was further than he or her mother had gotten educationally. (He failed to mention that they had supported Beth's brother through four years of college and a wedding.)

Anyway, Beth continued coming to church on Sundays and reporting her progress. She had helped a relative over the summer who cleaned houses for a living. That meant earning some money toward personal expenses during year one. Academically she had signed up for liberal arts courses rather than career preparation opportunities. She also began teaching a fifth and sixth grade Sunday School class which kept her studying the Bible and helping her students with everyday applications of Christian principles.

I had mentioned becoming an Associate of an order of Episcopalian nuns in Wisconsin, and Beth asked if she also could become an Associate. Since that would entail regular financial contributions, I offered instead to pass along the nuns' newsletters and other materials until she could afford to become an Associate. She agreed, but I wondered at her interest. My own reason for becoming an Associate was that it required having a spiritual rule of life with regular prayers and Bible study, a necessity for maintaining my demanding role as a single parent.

As she had in high school, Beth excelled in her college studies which pleased her Rotary sponsors. Near the end of her second year, Beth confided that she had decided to join the Order of nuns after graduation and become a nun herself. Her limp had evidently prevented her having dates and if marriage was not a possibility for her, being a nun would make her a "bride of Christ," an even better future. She would not be lonely and would be respected. Besides, her parents had warned her that she was "to move out on your own" after graduation from junior college and she had nowhere to go.

Beth seemed determined, so I agreed to write a letter of recommendation to the Mother Superior investigating the possibility and procedures. My heart hurt for Beth thinking of the pain she must have felt to watch couples everywhere, but never having a boyfriend herself. Probably this was true because she couldn't dance and was a brilliant student, both things off-putting to young men of her age. Perhaps her proposed course—to seek her place in an all-female environment, to love and be loved by Our Lord himself was the right path for Beth.

The same night of the day Beth requested I find out what was required to become an Anglican nun, I wrote to the Mother Superior recommending Beth become a postulant. I pointed out her excellent academic record and church work, not neglecting to mention her limp which did not handicap her for routine activities.

Mother Agnes' reply was affirmative, suggesting Beth come for two weeks in early summer as a visitor to experience the nuns' weekly round of prayer services, meals, work, and study. If that confirmed her feeling of being called to become a nun, then they could arrange for her to enter and begin the process of leaving the world behind as a postulant.

Beth was jubilant, but when she told her parents, they tried to talk her out of such a radical lifestyle which would not result in any grandchildren for them and was just "too Catholic," an affront to their fundamentalist Protestant beliefs.

"If you persist in doing this, your mother and I will disown you!"

"Just let me visit for two weeks," Beth pleaded. "Maybe I won't like it. One way or another, I'll be gone by fall."

Reluctantly, her father agreed, feeling certain that Beth would become disillusioned and give up her impractical plans. Those of us church folks in whom Beth had confided prayed for guidance for her before she reported in July for the Visitors Two Weeks at Mount Mercy Nunnery outside of Ripon, Wisconsin. I drove her up since I had attended spiritual retreats there and knew the way, not that her father had offered.

Beth was excited and nervous as we approached the great stone complex, but the sight of welcoming nuns in traditional black and white habits cordially introducing themselves calmed her.

"Some day before too long, I want to be dressed like that," she whispered to me as we turned and climbed the short flight of steps into a reception area. About a dozen women of varying ages were enjoying tea and getting acquainted…other participants just curious or like Beth, considering becoming nuns. I put Beth's single small suitcase in the designated area, gave her a farewell blessing and hug, then left.

Every day the next two weeks I prayed for Beth. Finally it was time to travel back north to retrieve her.

"Well?" I inquired as soon as we were homeward bound.

"Yes, oh YES," Beth replied and talked practically nonstop all the way describing living in a solitary cell, responding to bells every few hours to summon one to a service, meal, or other prescribed activity.

"I had Holy Communion every day and learned to sing the responses," she enthused. "There is no unnecessary talking outside of the evening social hour," she continued. "That was hard and the community bathrooms with toilets, sinks, and showers were at the end of each dormitory hall. That took some getting used to…taking your towel and washcloth with you for a nightly shower."

"There was even a prayer service at two a.m., but we visitors weren't required to attend it like the Regulars." On and on she spoke of how peaceful and stable the nuns lived with their set routines and sisterly relationships…of the beauty of their services with chanting and short sermons called homilies.

"Last night I told the nun in charge of the Visitation that I had definitely decided to join the Order for the rest of my life," Beth proclaimed.

I hoped it was the right choice, reminding her that it would alienate her family and mean leaving practically everything she owned behind.

"I know, but I think becoming a nun is worth it. This fall I would have been out on my own anyway. The nun told me to fill out some forms she gave me and mail them back. There's a new class of women preparing to become Postulants—the beginning rank—starting September first. That would give me six weeks to finish with my job, close out my bank account, and give away my belongings. Please say you're glad for me, Lara."

"If you want it enough for your life's work, Beth, then I AM glad for you," I assured her. "If you need a ride up to report for training, I'll be happy to take you."

"You're such a sweetheart, Lara, for always being an older person I can talk with who really cares."

"You're an easy girl to love, Beth. Now, who do you think we can approach to take over as teacher of your Sunday School class?"

The remainder of the ride was consumed with her plans, and I gave her a hug when I helped her unload her suitcase from the car in front of her home. The following Sunday a much quieter Beth than her usual sunny-self confirmed that her family opposed her plans and told her not to count on visiting them once she embarked upon what they called "throwing your life away."

I provided what comfort I could, inviting her to have lunch with my gang at a local restaurant that served bowls of peanuts and nutcrackers for throwing shells on the floor while you waited for your food order. My kids enjoyed the informal atmosphere and I could sit still and banter with them after the more formal church setting. Afterward we gave her a ride home so she wouldn't have to wait for and take a bus.

The last Sunday in August the church had a special cake at Coffee Hour in honor of Beth's leaving. She had given most of her clothing to the Salvation Army Thrift Store, her books and recordings to the local library. Her summer job had ended and she had closed her bank account. Proudly she told me that she would have six hundred dollars to donate to the Order when she entered. We arranged for me to pick her up early on September first and we would have brunch (my treat) on the way north.

When I arrived on September first, Beth was waiting on the porch with a small suitcase. It seems that her family said their good-byes last evening. She explained briefly. "I cried, Lara, but they didn't change my plans. Let's go.

As we got farther along the highway, Beth cheered up. By day's end she'd be in her new home beginning training for the life she'd chosen. Over lunch she enthusiastically described the progressive uniform changes called "habits" she would be wearing from now on in the three stages until becoming a full-fledged nun.

Upon arriving at the nunnery, I parked and went in with Beth who was whisked away after a brief hug and kiss. Before leaving I explained to the Mother Superior about how Beth's family disapproved of her career choice and if Beth needed some assistance or reports on her progress should be sent to me as her sponsor. To facilitate that, I gave her my calling card with contact information.

I expected very little more social contact with Beth, but hoped all would go well with her training. Imagine my surprise when the following June I received a phone call from the Nunnery requesting that I come and collect Beth—that she had been the "ring-leader of a number of pranks by current trainees" and was therefore "no longer deemed suitable for the very disciplined, enclosed life of a nun."

Although it meant canceling several commitments, I arranged to go north the following day, a Saturday, to retrieve Beth. She explained on the way back to River City, dressed in the same clothes she'd worn on September's happier trip, that "Those women just don't have a good sense of humor. Maybe it's for the best I'm leaving."

The culminating trick they'd played on the older nuns was to turn off the lights in the Community Shower Room late one night while Mother Superior was taking her usual solitary shower. "You could hear her screaming two halls away," gloated Beth with a laugh.

"Oh, Beth," I moaned, but had to grin at the picture she painted of the dismayed elegant head of the Order. I was reminded of the heroine of the movie "The Sound of Music" when the nuns sang about wondering what to do with a girl like Maria. Perhaps Beth also had too high spirits to be locked away from society. But having pretty much burned all bridges with her family, what would her future hold? Even if her parents forgave her, they had already eliminated the wall to her former bedroom to extend their living room, so there was now no room for her at their home.

"You are welcome to stay at our place for the summer while Susan is working as a nurse's aide down in Unity," I offered.

"You're a life saver!" she gratefully accepted. "Maybe I could work as a shelver in your library?"

"You'd need to be registered for at least one course," I cautioned, "to be eligible for student employment. But we'll check that out on Monday. Tomorrow you'll see all your old friends at the church."

My mind raced as we rode on toward River City. One more place at the table was OK, but Beth would need clothing (probably Salvation Army Thrift Store stuff), transportation, cosmetics, student supplies, etc. to start over. Previously she had wanted to transfer to River City College's four year program to complete a B.A. degree, but now had no personal resources. "Dear Lord, please help me to help Beth," I prayed silently.

Martha agreed to share her small bedroom with Beth, Ron was headquartered in the basement, and Patty could sleep with me when she came for weekends from Swerlin. On Monday Beth rode with me when I went into work as Public Services Librarian. She then walked across campus to the Admissions Office to have them request a transcript of her junior college course work and to fill out applications for admittance and for scholarship assistance. They could also help her line out the courses she would need to enroll in to earn her degree.

By five p.m., time to ride home with me, Beth was quite hopeful about her new future. Because her junior college record was so excellent, her Admissions representative would recommend her for a full two-year scholarship—summer, fall, and spring. If granted, that would take care of tuition until her graduation.

As a student, Beth could hold a library job as a shelver with flexible hours so she could commute with me. The pay was not large, but would probably cover textbooks and incidentals as long as I provided free room and board. All of this amounted to much more than I had envisioned, but somehow I knew I had been selected to be Beth's friend and Biblical "neighbor", so I agreed to her becoming a member of our household not only for the summer, but for the next two academic years.

Susan would be attending the University of Illinois and we'd manage somehow on vacations. I hoped my automatic annual raise would cover the larger food bills, and transportation costs would remain approximately the same. Once Beth obtained her degree, she would be equipped to get a job and earn her own upkeep.

The next morning I phoned Beth's Admissions advisor and thanked him for interceding on Beth's behalf and offered to act as a reference if one were needed for her scholarship.

"No need for that, Lara. As Admissions Department Head, I believe my recommendation will be enough. When I heard that you had taken her into your own home, I could hardly do less than advise her on the fastest route to her degree and arrange for scholarship assistance. I believe she'll make both of us very proud, Lara, for she is one of the best students I ever admitted. Bless you for all you are doing to welcome her back into the real world and academe."

"Let's just hope it all works out," I responded and hung up to resume regular duties. Since several of my senior library shelvers had graduated, I was able to offer Beth three hours per weekday in and around her course work or fifteen hours per week. Other shelvers would have to take care of evenings and weekends since Beth would need those to pursue her studies. I'd purchase lunch cards for the cafeteria and she'd take the rest of her meals with our family. In just one week after leaving the convent, Beth could count on housing, a part-time job, transportation, and scholarships to cover tuition to complete her BA degree.

That is how Beth became my dependent for a little, but important time. She went on after graduation to earn a graduate degree in Medieval History at the University of Indiana. We went to her wedding to a fellow graduate student in the University's Episcopal Chapel just two years after leaving us. Her limp had obviously not kept her from dating him, and her future was promising. We WERE very proud of Beth.

CHAPTER SIX

The Gifted One Gives Me Fits

Daughter in seesaw competition

I don't know why it took me by surprise that my second daughter Marsha, third in line, would turn out to be such an unruly teen. She had always exhibited tremendous independence from the time she began learning to dress herself and talk. Her "I dood it myself" became a familiar watch word around our house.

She was a beautiful blonde and very petite like the tiny women in her father's family. From her birth she was the darling of the Caring Hospital nursery, for most blondes are not born blonde as she was and she had suffered little trauma during her quick delivery, so her complexion was not as red as most newborns.

Despite the favorable attention her doll-like appearance brought her, Martha let me know that I could keep all those frilly dresses. She preferred pants and practical play clothes. Only for Sunday church could I persuade her to dress in a dress.

Since Martha had learned to read before she entered kindergarten, I approached a parent's conference with her teacher without a single qualm. Imagine my surprise when her teacher complained that Martha "is entirely too competitive. Why, she even has to be first in the lunch line."

It seems that Martha's assertiveness was not her teacher's only aggravation; there had also developed a serious personality conflict problem because Martha asked every day if she couldn't transfer to the other kindergarten class down the hall. (Since Martha's teacher was also the wife of the Superintendent of Schools, and I had three children and another one coming up for that school system, this also constituted a major social crisis for the Vicar's family.) When queried, Martha explained that the other kindergarten teacher had long blonde hair, was young and full of fun. I sympathized, but explained she was stuck for the rest of this year and instructed her not to alienate her teacher further by ever asking again for a transfer.

Agile and quick, Martha more than made up for her slight build with courage and fine motor coordination. At breakfast one morning she announced that next month on her seventh birthday she was going to beat up the big boy who teased and annoyed her at the school bus stop. She had determined in her heart of hearts that she would be strong and brave enough to confront him on that day.

Fr. Patrick and I tried to let the children handle their own disputes, so this was the first we'd heard about this evidently chronic problem. Her birthday came and we waited for a report. Ron carried the news since he'd made himself late by hiding and watching the confrontation.

"Mom, she was fantastic! Martha just tied into him like a little whirlwind, kicking and punching, and shouting at him to 'leave me alone!' It took him by surprise and he agreed with 'OK ... OK, kid, let up!' I bet he'll think twice before he annoys her again."

Martha was smiling with smug satisfaction when she arrived home. We were all looking forward to her birthday supper and cake, for we knew it was a significant day in Martha's life.

Fr. Patrick had wanted a boy-child to share his love of baseball, but after Patty arrived, he decided to settle for the athletic Martha as his entry into the world of Little League. Traditionally the League was all boys and male coaches, but Patrick thought that if he could turn Martha into a super pitcher, the League might make an exception. Martha was an apt student of the American game. Patrick and she practiced throwing, pitching, and batting on a regular schedule... around listening to the real games on radio or watching the few carried on television.

Martha turned out to be a great pitcher—much more control and swifter than her contemporaries in vacant lot play. Patrick worked up a petition to admit her to Little League which most of the boys in her grade at school signed.

One night when Ron and I pulled in—late as usual from our River City commuting—there was company in our living room. Two large men representing the Little League were explaining to my petite Martha and her red-faced father trainer why neither of them was to be permitted to join. "It was a vote of the present coaches who don't want changes," they said and hurried away to more pleasant tasks.

No one ate much supper. We ached for Martha's disappointment and the dashed hopes of her father-coach. I marveled that she didn't cry, but she explained, "Tough guys don't cry!" Her parting shot as she left to feed her bird with the injured wing was, "So let them lose!' This incident added fuel to my growing desire to leave Swerlin.

When the children and I finally did leave to live full-time in the River City apartment, Martha qualified for the Academy, a gifted middle school. While there she conceived the goal of doing something that would qualify her to be listed in the "Guiness Book of World Records" and settled upon setting a new world's record for consecutive hours spent on a seesaw. The rules specified certain half-hour breaks for meals and bathroom needs set by the current holder of the forty-eight-hour record.

Martha enlisted the help of her classmates and teacher, and I gained permission from the Park District for use of their seesaw closest to the street entrance for this event and notified the Guiness people about Martha's project.

A fifty-hour schedule of 2-hour rotating classmate partners was set with their parents' consent and cooperation in delivering each one to the park on time and taking their youngster home again in the Friday five p.m. to Sunday seven p.m. time frame. 'Quite a complex organizational effort for a middle school student! Each student and responsible parent signed in on a master list to verify their participation. I would be there the entire time to furnish soda anytime plus hand food and to provide escorted restroom trips for Martha during breaks.

Friday night and Saturday morning went as anticipated, Martha's excitement buoying all the rest of us. By Saturday afternoon I noticed that her exposed skin was pink from exposure to the sun and suggested sunscreen was in order at her next scheduled break. "Don't bother, Mom. It doesn't hurt," was Martha's response and back she climbed to resume her ups and downs.

By Saturday evening Martha was showing signs of fatigue—slower and fewer lifts and descents as the hours wore on. I was also very weary but determined to support my spunky girl through to the seven p.m. Sunday goal. But by noon Sunday Martha's sunburn was hot and red, her breathing erratic and I worried she might fall off the seesaw. She would have if I had not caught her leaning over too far and declared a halt to the entire attempt because of probable sunstroke.

I rushed her home while her teacher called the homes of those remaining on the schedule to announce the end of Martha's attempt to set a new seesaw record. For two days Martha rested on her bed scantily clothed and drinking lots of cool liquids with soothing lotions on her sunburns.

"I should have worn more protective clothing and listened to you about sunscreen," she lamented. "I made a fool of myself, didn't I?"

"Darling," I responded, "life is full of ups and downs. It's win some, lose some. This was a great attempt and you learned a lot about how to organize and what your physical limits are. There'll be other tasks ahead when you can succeed because of what you learned from this one."

To make up for not being able to join Little League baseball in Swerlin, I enrolled Martha in a gymnastics class. This more suited to her petite and agile frame. How she enjoyed balancing and flipping in this new and challenging environment! Many an evening I sat in the gymn's bleachers watching Martha practice her more advanced movements. Shortly she became one of the most skillful students.

At the end of two years of lessons and progressive routines in local competitions, Martha was slated to perform in Hawaii with a handful of other gifted River City gymnasts at the World Age Games. I raised the three-hundred dollars each gymnast was required to contribute toward trip expenses by selling our entire camping outfit—tent, sleeping bags, coolers, lamps, grill, etc. We were probably at the end of camping days anyway. The sacrifice was well worth it when Martha made us proud by placing twenty-first in the world for her age group.

As she approached the end of grade school, Martha took up

with two girlfriends—Tammy and Terrie. The three were practically inseparable—teen-aged "outsiders" coming from less affluent families. Tammy's single mother lived in a trailer park near the airport, and Terrie's folks lived two streets over from our home in an old, somewhat rundown house. Also, the three made higher grades which did not endear the trio with their contemporaries.

One frigid February day I received a phone call at work from Terrie's folks telling me that our three girls had run away from home instead of going to school. Could I come to their home right away to confer with an investigating policeman? I sped over to join Tammy's mom also there and found out that both Terrie and Tammy had run away before. This time the police would arrest and hold them until their parents could confer with a social worker about appropriate punishment. Since Martha had never behaved like this before, I asked that she be returned home and I would deal with the aftermath. Returning to work, I stayed close to the phone awaiting further word.

Martha already had a bad cold and I worried she might be risking pneumonia. About two p.m. I was informed that the three runaways had been apprehended at a laundromat two towns south of River City. However, Martha had sassed the arresting officer, so she also had been arrested and would be returned to the River City jail with the other two. I would be called later about when to come down to the jail for Martha's and my appointment with a social worker.

Impatiently I called back to the jail when I was ready to leave work. No appointment time was yet available. By seven p.m. I was getting quite frantic when word finally came that Martha and I would have the last appointment at nine p.m.

Single parents are often on the defensive, so I dressed carefully in heels, business suit, and fur jacket hoping that our interviewer would realize Martha came from a proper home. I still had no idea why Martha had run away. At the appointed time an officer escorted my daughter in. She appeared tired, bedraggled and anxious without shoelaces or belt, but glad to see and sit next to me.

"Why did you run away? Was it something I did or didn't do?" I asked her.

"No, Mom, but you know how irresponsible Tammy and Terrie can sometimes be. I couldn't let them set off by themselves." I caught the social worker hiding a grin behind her hand as I digested that incredible explanation. Gradually as we spoke further with the social worker, I realized that the police officers had indeed instilled in Martha a firm determination to never again go against the law. Having to surrender her belt and shoelaces and to be locked up for long solitary hours behind bars had taught Martha a good lesson. On our way home she asked if we could stop at a fast food place to get something to eat—she had also suffered hunger as part of that lesson.

Two major events were associated with Martha's sixteenth birthday in 1979. She quit school because her eighth-grade guidance counselor had told her and Tammy that according to their Intelligence Quotient test scores, they were already operating at a twelfth grade level. (Fortunately for him I never discovered his identity.) To their teen age minds there was no reason to attend four years of high school if they were already at a twelfth-grade level intellectually. I was devastated, but insisted that Martha get a work permit and a job. She was not going to sit around home and get into trouble.

One of the few firms willing to employ young people with work permits was Notable Toys where workers assembled small toys. Tammy followed Martha's lead, so I would deliver Martha and Tammy to their jobs at eight a.m. and retrieve them at five p.m. weekdays. Wages were meager, but the girls were at least under supervision during working hours. One evening while Martha helped with clearing the kitchen after supper, she commented,"You know, Mom, some of those people at work have been putting those little toys together for twenty years!"

Sensing I'd never have a better chance, I replied, "Well, that's because they never got a high school diploma, Martha." I heard her catch her breath, but no words came.

Not long after that exchange I learned that River City Business College downtown would enroll high school dropouts. When I queried Martha about this possibility, she leaped at the chance to leave the boring factory job. Her new and practical studies in typing, bookkeeping, and shorthand challenged her and kept her occupied until she was old enough to have graduated the usual way. Since schools were reimbursed according to attendance, no one was permitted to take the High School Equivalency Test before then.

River City Business College even offered a preparatory course for students ahead of taking that test. When Martha took the test, she aced it and was enabled to enter River City College's next freshman class. Once again my second daughter was back on track educationally.

Socially, Martha also worried me. She and Tammy spent their spare time with a mixed group of hippy-type guys and girls who used drugs. I let the band practice in our basement...anything to keep Martha close to home. Her complexion turned grayish, and I was concerned about her dating John who rode about on a motorcycle. He was the most clean-cut of the young men in the group, but wasn't the type I would have chosen for Martha.

The second happening on Martha's sixteenth birthday was John's gift to her of a Great Dane puppy. When she came to happily show me this canine addition to our family, I wasn't sure what type this large puppy was, not knowing that Great Danes' ears aren't naturally pointed and are surgically altered. I did realize that it would have a large appetite and add seriously to our already strained food budget. We named the puppy Zechariah as the last and best of our dogs. Zack turned out to be a marvelous animal—intelligent, loving and protective.

Because of his size he couldn't fit into my Volkswagen "bug", so we went shopping secondhand car lots for a second vehicle large enough to carry Zack. We bought the only one both large enough and cheap enough to serve the purpose—an old black hearse. It probably horrified our neighbors, but we never had to lock it when

Zack was aboard. One growl from him would guarantee the vehicle's safety. Besides, who but us would want such a vehicle?

The deciding factor for Martha's coming to a decision about and swearing off drugs occurred one night when I got a phone call from her at two a.m. Since she had gone to bed at home around ten o'clock, I was astonished.

"Can you come get me, Mom?" Martha asked in a quivering voice.

"Where are you?"

"I'm in a telephone booth in front of the Sleepytime Motel in and she named a town about ten miles south of River City."

"OK," I agreed, 'Stay right there. I'll get dressed and be coming right away." I lost no time scrambling into my clothes and speeding south. Sure enough; there was Martha shivering and without her shoes. She stumbled to my car and got in.

"Please don't ask me any questions, Mom," she pleaded as I turned the car around and headed for home. "I'll never do anything like this again... ever. I'm going to get clean, honest. Thanks so much for coming, Mom."

Her tear-stained face hurt my heart. "I love you and want nothing but the best for you, hon," I replied. "But you have to do your part. You know what I mean." And I let that be the end of our talk about this adventure.

About six months later Martha told me that she and Tammy (Terrie was going steady with someone and had opted out of this next caper.) were going to Las Vegas to seek their fortunes. She assumed I'd be glad to see her leave. On the contrary, I had experienced some of what could happen to a young girl on her own in a large city when I left home at age nineteen and went to Philadelphia for a year. There was no way she'd have my permission to go off to Las Vegas; I told her I'd have her brought back as a runaway since she was not yet eighteen years old.

Martha's earlier time in the River City jail as a runaway did not bear repeating. Although she threw a temper tantrum, I remained firm and Tammy left alone for Las Vegas. Word got back to Martha that Tammy was working for one of the numerous quick wedding chapels, but before long the news about Tammy became tragic. She got into trouble with the law several times and finally had to serve a prison term.

Tammy had a baby while in prison and wrote asking Martha to raise the child. Both John and I counseled against establishing such a close and continuing tie with Tammy. The upshot was that Tammy's mother, the infant's grandmother, would raise the child. I refrained from any "I told you so's," grateful that God had led me to refuse Martha permission to go to Las Vegas with Tammy.

With Tammy gone, Martha settled down to dating John who had also sworn off drugs after a close call from an overdose. Back then he was part of a motorcycle gang that ran afoul of the law more than once. Finally, a judge gave John the option of leaving Illinois or serving time in prison.

John's sister in Denver offered her help and John asked Martha to accompany him into exile. Since Martha had passed her eighteenth birthday, it was her decision to make. That's how, on very short notice, Martha left with John, Zack, their hastily packed clothes and other belongings in the old hearse for Denver. It would be three years before John and Martha returned, married, and moved into a decrepit old farmhouse with two acres of land southwest of River City which his sister and father helped them purchase.

Martha returned to River City College for her B.S. degree utilizing my family benefit and added Certified Public Accounting training. Meanwhile their only child, a girl named "Sarah" was born. John had learned carpentry skills from his father, so around regular wage-earning jobs, he gradually repaired and restored their small house.

No longer did John run with any motorcycle gang, but he did enjoy an occasional solo ride upon a very expensive customized motorcycle left to him by a friend who died very young. When John developed back problems from heavy lifting on the job, he returned to alcohol to alleviate the pain. This created marital problems for which they sought professional counseling at my urging. Some progress was slowly made.

By now Martha was working as a CPA with a large River City firm and earning more than John did which bothered him. In their detached two-car garage with a large office behind it on their property John turned the office into a recording studio where he earned a bit by recording local bands and soloists. Young Sarah was growing and proved to be a bright student from kindergarten forward. I kept her overnight every Saturday and took her to church and Sunday School every Sunday with me to provide Martha and John a date night.

John's drinking finally led to a diagnosis of severe liver problems. He had to quit alcohol "cold turkey" and subsequently was placed on a liver transplant waiting list. Fortunately, Martha carried family medical coverage at work. Many patients die awaiting compatible transplants, but John was one of the fortunate ones whose liver matched the liver of a young man killed in an automobile accident. This medical crisis stretching over two years cemented John and Martha's marriage especially since it eradicated John's alcoholism once and for all.

They still live on their two acres which is bounded on one side by a small stream where wildlife come to drink. Although officially retired, John still does some recording jobs. He finally sold his motorcycle to help provide Sarah a car for college at Eastern Indiana University.

Martha bumped into the proverbial "glass ceiling" at work when a young male CPA whom she had mentored was promoted to partner over her despite her eight years of experience. It provoked her into leaving that firm to establish her own business in a storefront in River City's downtown section.

The money she had inherited after her father's death helped with office renovations and online capabilities. She joined the River City Chamber of Commerce and several other organizations for networking possibilities. A one-day-a-week job with the local hospice group paid enough to cover her basic expenses, and a friend volunteered to become her receptionist. Martha would see clients by appointment in and around her civic commitments. She was asked to present the newest changes made by the IRS to income taxes for the local CPAs, probably because she had more time to prepare such a program than her more established accounting friends. Her excellent analysis, however, led to her being offered an Assistant Professorship at River City University. She manages both her teaching responsibilities and private practice.

John took early retirement and undertook full responsibility for their two dogs and large yard. He will be on anti-rejection meds the rest of his life and being his own boss suits his reformed temperament. The small private recording studio behind the garage still yields some extra income.

Several years back John invented and patented a trailer hitch to connect a motorcycle behind a car, a hitch he hopes to have manufactured in River City and promote sales thereafter. Having their own businesses in cooperation with one another bodes well for a stable marriage and future.

Need for a larger vehicle

CHAPTER SEVEN

Lessening the Parenting Load

With my professional life going along well despite large needs to meet my financial commitments and my personal life devastated by a second divorce, I desperately reached out to any reassuring and friendly help I could find. One visit to the local chapter of the most logical network—Parents Without Partners—convinced me that those folks were most interested in pairing again. 'Something about the way the lucky women clutched the arm and attention of the few males present and the wary stares of the remaining hopefuls. What I felt I needed was a true friendship network where we could safely socialize while we healed from divorce and could trade some unaccustomed duties and expertise without emotional strings attached. Not finding that sort of group, typically I organized one—The Parenting Singles.

One feature of this new group was a monthly newsletter which listed possible weekly social outings with costs and reservation deadlines. Naturally I listed events I wanted to attend and restaurants I wanted to try in the company of others who were not part of the customary couple scene. We also kept a listing of skills and babysitting hours traded.

One iron-clad rule was no pairing at any of our sponsored events which might make a single feel even more lonely. If individuals wanted to establish liaisons outside our sphere, so be it... but never at Episcopal Singles' events. A side benefit was a hotline I provided for those middle of-the-night blues situations. Only occasionally did anyone call to disturb my sleep, but many said that the possibility of having someone to call and talk to at two a.m. helped them tough it through some crises at night.

Early on in my search for a church my four offspring and I visited St. Stephen's, the smallest Episcopal mission in Lonely Park just north of River City. Since my former husband's best friend was rector of the big "yuppie" congregation on the fashionable east side of River City, I avoided that Episcopal stronghold. The traditional downtown church, "Emanuel" was headed by an arch conservative who had forced my female faculty friend off their vestry which caused her to leave the Episcopal Church. I needed no additional battles to fight.

Besides; the first time we attended St. Stephen's the teddy-bear of a vicar with a magnificent baritone voice made us extremely welcome. (I later learned that be had studied at the University of Indiana's opera school.) At the coffee hour after that first service he announced that their organist was moving away and asked, "Anyone here play the organ?" My son, God love him, volunteered me. I'd taken a few lessons with the Catholic organist in Swerlin, but was not very proficient. However, since no one else could play, the newly vacated post was all mine beginning the following Sunday. Ron may have been impressed with my playing of hymns, but my skills were rudimentary. However, I was worth as much as my non-existent salary. Every week I practiced on the piano at home, then on the organ Wednesday evenings after midweek services and on Saturdays. Because I was so nervous, I'd take two tranquilizers on Sunday mornings to keep my bands from shaking on the keys. Week after week I found new mistakes to make, and the old pedal organ contributed its share of trauma when it would stick on a note...it's called siphoning.

This continued for two years until a more accomplished organist was located who would play for a very modest fee. My organist days did distract me from other interior demons which threatened occasionally to overwhelm my otherwise capable-appearing exterior.

What a close-knit community St. Stephen's was for the most part. We really kept the Biblical injunction to "rejoice with those who rejoice and weep with those who weep." Those good people helped me raise the children with prayers, excellent Christian education programs, and regular duties to perform. The potlucks and annual spaghetti supper were legendary. It was a church family, and since my own family was so far away in Pennsylvania, I leaned into these church relationships with great gratitude.

Fr. Parker was also a gourmet cook and talented story teller, so be became a favorite extra guest at our home for holiday celebrations. His sweet potato souffle was "to die for" as Ron expressed it. One notable birthday dinner went on and on for hours as Fr. Parker and my elderly Jewish dentist friend, Maurice Henton, traded jokes about priests and rabbis.

In 1991—on Mother's Day weekend—Fr. Parker in his most imperious manner commanded that I treat myself to a Cursillo Weekend. This proved to be a renewal weekend where Christian love and worship became tangible with contagious music, sincere life witnessing, notes and small gifts from Cursillistas I'd never met, greetings from Cursillo movements far away, excellent food, and gracious details such as hand-decorated napkins. I'd never felt so pampered and special.

The follow-up effect was that I learned to drive around Cranston in order to continue to associate with these enthusiastic Cursillistas. Eventually I served six years on the CHEC (Cranston Episcopal Cursillo) Secretariat, wearing out one Volkswagon in the process. It was somewhat disillusioning behind the scenes—people were just people with some of the same faults and foibles I'd found in other groups. But prayer and good will helped us over many rough spots. Changes in priests at St. Stephen's and the other two Episcopal churches in the River City area weakened this renewal thrust.

I was elected to be the first female Bishop's Warden at St. Stephen's. This was no doubt because no man wanted the job. The building program had soured with the contractor close to completing our community center/parish hall addition, but we lacked the wherewithal to make his last payment.

Two years before this the national church had announced a

push for expansion of Episcopal outreach facilities. I volunteered to write a grant proposal for St. Stephen's because we needed a parish hall where we could host more and larger groups. Although our leadership doubted anything would come of it, they gave me permission to apply. When my proposal became the only one from our deanery, then one of two from the Diocese of Cranston, some interest in my proposal to house an elderly day care in cooperation with Community Services for the Lonely Park area surfaced. When we were awarded the building grant and construction began, members who had not participated in drawing up the proposal started demanding changes. The women insisted that there must be a window over the sink and the restrooms in the foyer must be made smaller so a small coatroom could be added, etc. Of course, all changes added to the building's cost. I felt responsible for having gotten St.Stephen's into this bind.

Finally, in desperation I offered to take out a second mortgage on my home to cover the contractor's shortage. But God moved hearts of the men on the Bishop's Committee. They refused to let this single mother undertake such a financial burden and among themselves raised what was needed. For years there were cars parked every day of the week in the parking lot testifying to St. Stephen's outreach programs.

My oldest, Susan, graduated from the University of Illinois in Nursing and moved to Unity to become a full-fledged nurse at Caring Clinic, the same hospital where her father was Head of the Anesthesiology Department and where she'd gotten her practical experience summers. Caring Clinic administrators were pleased to recruit such a proven person, and her father was very proud to have her on the same staff.

Ron had finally gotten his driver's license and one course short of obtaining his four-year degree from Northern Indiana University (Statistics), he joined the Air Force. Since he was stationed in Montana, that left Marsha at home with Patty visiting weekends when she was not tied up with high school activities once or twice a month.

Patty was dating David Filler all through high school. His family was traditionally military, so Dave enlisted right after graduating from high school. When he was stationed in England and Patty was attending Higgins Junior College in Fanville, they wrote constantly. She cleaned doctors' offices at night to pay for dormitory privileges. Since Father Patrick had moved to Sterling to teach at the junior college there, Patty lived with me.

As soon as Patty had earned her two-year degree and Dave had returned to the United States, they married. Fr. Patrick performed their ceremony at St. James in Swerlin, and the newlyweds began together to complete his twenty-year military career.

The yard work became oppressive with Ron gone and Marsha a very reluctant mower, so I began paying my neighbor on the uphill side to do the large side lawn and "way back" right along with his lawn while he was zipping around with his riding mower. What a relief—to pare the outside chores to the more manageable front and fenced in back yard. I paid him quarterly in and around car insurance and other big bills.

Having completed my term as Bishop's Warden and righted St. Stephen's with lots of prayer, open meetings, private cajolings, and a bit of diocesan assistance, I enjoyed some small peace. As a single parent or parent at all, I've learned to lean into such relatively quiet periods, for crises are certain to interrupt before very long. In this case, I arrived home from the annual family reunion to find Marsha preparing to leave with Zack and John for Denver where his sister lives. It seems that John had gotten into some fracas while drinking and been told by a judge that he must leave Illinois within ten days or face jail time. Marsha and John had been dating for several years, but although going steady, they had not married.

Since Marsha had come of age—eighteen in Illinois—I had no recourse this time except to let them go. I did let them sell off all their excess and my belongings still in the house after I'd moved into the apartment in my converted garage. Proceeds would give them travel money and start-up funds.

For me it meant an unexpected, premature "empty nest" for which I was totally unprepared emotionally. While I helped them with their hasty departure that week, I was trying to teach an Elder Hostel class on the Black Hawk War. Unfortunately, most of the elderly participants were from Wisconsin and not open to considering the initial rout of White troops by Black Hawk's warriors in our area nor the wholesale massacre of Indians retreating across the Mississippi River near Wisconsin that the final defeat became.

I'd amassed official Army reports and contemporary eye witness accounts, but between my distraction about Marsha's departure and the participants' inbred disbelief, I received the only negative teaching evaluations of my long career. Somehow it seemed appropriate that Black Hawk and I were losing the last of our dreams for his homeland and my "Bonnell Refuge" the same week. At least no one died when the Denver-bound hearse with Zack aboard departed. A great desolation descended upon me, however, when I reentered the deserted house to list all that needed to be cleaned, repaired and painted before I could possibly rent it.

"No family left—I'm all alone" kept tearing at my heart, especially at night. My prayers followed the travelers until I learned of their safe arrival and successful fresh start in Denver. Eventually the work of getting the house ready to rent brought sound sleep at night. I adjusted to life in my small cottage apartment and threw myself in my spare time into peace and justice activities. These included being on the Board of Community Services, the River City Hunger Walk, Peace Studies at River City College, Amnesty International, the Jane Addams Society and her Women's International League for Peace and Freedom, and the Women's History Month Steering Committee besides being a Lay Reader at St. Stephen's.

It is amazing how much time, money, and energy parenting requires. Not until released from most of that did I appreciate what an overwhelming preoccupation parenting is. "Once a parent, always a parent" the wise old saying goes. One continues to pray and worry about their offspring whether they are ten or forty years old. It's decidedly more fun being a grandparent when you can love, enjoy, spoil and then send the precious next generation along home.

CHAPTER EIGHT

Suitors and Other Prospects

Although I had been married and divorced twice, I was not totally reconciled to remaining a single parent. There needed to be healing time, of course—"at least two years" I counseled other singles. Somehow my having survived two divorces made me an authority on divorce-recovery... that and like a typical librarian... having read everything I could find on the subject.

I had male friends on the River City College faculty, but only one real marriage prospect. We dated a couple of times, but he looked over my family and property, then honestly told me that he'd been through a lot of child-rearing and property maintenance already. He was trying to beat a drinking problem and was reluctant to take on again the very things he believed had driven him to drink before. His Irish humor and frankness kept us friends, but I needed helpful commitment. Whenever I tried to become dependent upon another human being, God whisked the possibility away sooner or later. When would I learn that the Lord is truly a jealous God and wants primary dependence to be upon Him?

There was another later arrangement—not entirely satisfactory, but filling part of my huge emotional void. Like many single women, I fell into the trap of indulging in an affair. It consisted of brief sexual interludes with an older married man who though sexually deprived, had no intention of divorcing his wealthy wife. We would tryst in his car on a deserted road or in inclement weather by prearrangement at a motel on Saturday morning (after I... never he... had stopped by to check in on Friday evening to disarray the bed to foil the housekeeping staff). If I was late arriving or one of us was prevented from coming, things became very strained between us.

Guilt and fear of disclosure dogged the entire duration. When one of us was hospitalized, there was no way to show support. Travel separations could not be bridged by letters—too risky to commit anything in writing although both of us were basically writers. A few passionate, but anonymous poems resulted, and our liaison kept each of us from that black despair of being attractive to no one special.

Birthday and Christmas gifts were surreptitiously passed, but the accompanying cards were unsigned.

As time passed, we knew we were pushing the odds of being discovered, and increased security measures wore on both of us. Numerous times I called the whole affair off, but after a time of painful separation, we'd agree to "meet and talk" which usually resulted in our happily falling into one another's arms. Knowing just how to please and titillate the other, we would gratefully extend our clandestine relationship.

It became clearer to me that this man was an addiction and a dangerous one. My conscience destroyed peace of mind and my selfesteem was being undermined at the cost of brief pleasurable encounters. That's addiction with a capital "A" to say nothing of the capital "A" for adultery. Double sin and not enough will power to break the addictive cycle. As with all overwhelming things in my life, I finally (a part of me still reluctant) placed this holdout area before God and implored help to overcome the sexual addiction.

Then I waited with relief and curiosity to see how things would change. A long separation without any possible safe communication threw me onto my own resources. I learned how well life could proceed without the weekly trysts and their attendant guilt. But wary of my vulnerability and because of other aborted endings, I refused to meet my former lover anywhere alone.

He was quite confident that time apart with his circling close would work its usual weakening of my resolve. I took things one refusal at a time, for he still was both an attractive man and I knew how superb a lover. He undoubtedly still was, but only occasionally did I let myself see him and then at a distance.

An unexpected suitor materialized about this time—a very nice, clean younger man whose mother was a friend. Abe was a mathematician who taught at a Catholic preparatory school in the Cranston area, but visited his folks in River City on weekends. Women his own age found Abe a bit strange... terribly clean cut, an informed classical music fan, and very religious. He had tried his vocation for a time in a Catholic monastery, then been in India for a year becoming a Buddhist maha.

We got along well, having long religious discussions and going to concerts, plays, and other cultural events together. Once we even attended his school's spring formal where we danced as much or more than the uniformed students and their dates in formals and corsages.

Unfortunately, my four children thought Abe was "weird" and said so regularly. He sent me a used studio piano in exchange for the engagement ring I decided against and returned. No doubt his folks were also relieved. The upshot was that I was now convinced it would be unwise to bring any male permanently on board my precarious leaky ship while carrying a cargo of demanding and super sensitive adolescents. Marriage would have to wait.

CHAPTER NINE

This Feminist Defies Fate

As so often happens, just when I had given up on romance and decided to just keep my own life and household in order, I met SOMEONE SPECIAL. It was early on a Saturday morning when I had loaded five washers with the week's laundry at the local Laundromat to save time and our temperamental septic system. I went next door to get a bite of breakfast at Denny's while the laundry washed. Hardly ever does anyone steal wet clothes and I'd be back in time to guard my driers.

As a single woman, I signaled my independence by leaving a seat at the counter open between the next person and myself. Just as I started to slide into the intended place that morning, I noticed that the counter in front of it was dirty and hastily moved over one. That fateful shift placed me next to a big fellow with a Southern accent. He had a wide smile and joked easily with our waitress. I mistook him for a traveling salesman, and we began to talk as strangers do.

Somehow the subject of divorce came up and he said that he was in the process of getting a divorce. Remember how that was an area of my personal expertise? Well, I advised him to give himself two full years to heal and become whole... then seek another mate. It was a pleasant and meaningful breakfast chat, and I glanced at my watch to discover the washers had been finished their last cycle for some time. I wished him well and gathered up my bill preparing to leave.

"Wait a minute... " said the stranger. "I'm Shawn Cantor and I run Cantor's Saddle Shop here in Rockford. I come here for breakfast on weekends. 'Hope to see you again."

I could feel myself blushing. I'd not expected to ever see this Southern gentleman again, so I'd told him things I wouldn't have volunteered otherwise. You can bet I beat a hasty retreat, but it had been an interesting conversation with a man who reminded me of Clark Gable, the handsome movie star. The memory hummed in my head all week. I felt like an infatuated school girl and tried to talk sense into myself all that ensuing week.

Next Saturday while the kids slept late as usual, I was up early and had the laundry down the hill and into those Laundromat machines in jig time. My heart pounded as I approached Denny's once more. Inside the door, my eyes swept the counter but found no Clark Gable look alike. I'm bad at remembering names and was too flustered to recall his. Part of me was relieved, but a larger part was disappointed.

Suddenly from a booth in the far corner came a loud drawled "You're late!" Shawn waved me over. This time before I belatedly left to tend the driers I'd agreed to let him take me to dinner that evening.

Saturday breakfasts and evening dates with Shawn became a regular, looked-forward-to custom.

His humor and wise advice helped me keep my perspective and sanity for my remaining child rearing years. He liked Marsha and had been through some rough years with his own daughter previously.

When I'd be in great despair, he would assure me that Marsha was made of "good stuff" and would pull out of her current tailspin. "Just be loving and patient," he advised. I kept reminding myself that "Early training tells... early training eventually tells!"

'Easy for Shawn to talk, but I saw my pretty girl's complexion turning gray and her eyes looking strange. I recalled how I got a frantic two a.m. phone call from her and went to retrieve her barefoot and trembling from another town when I had thought she was asleep at home. Marsha was such a sorry-looking sight that I didn't scold and she offered no explanation beyond, "I'm SO glad you came. Thanks, Mom!"

I hoped she'd learned a lesson and since there never was a similar incident, I guess she had.

After Marsha and John with Zack departed for Colorado, leaving my house vacant and their pregnant cat to arrange for flying out, I lapsed into a quiet, tilt-overload depression. Shawn kept me focusing on getting the house ready to rent and loaned me his handkerchief when I missed all the parental stuff too much. My small quarters in the converted garage were lonely and eating alone was hard.

Gradually I spent more and more time under the apple tree at Shawn's between customers at the Saddle Shop in his converted and expanded garage beside his two-story home on Swanee Avenue. We would have dessert and watch television together after the shop closed. We both hated to part to get some rest for the next day.

Shawn worked as brick and tile foreman for a commercial builder during the day and operated his Saddle Shop evenings and weekends. He had married a German woman while stationed in Europe during the Second World War, then brought her to this country as his war bride. It became more and more obvious to him that her main motive for marrying him was to get to the United States, not love for him. She and their only child, a daughter named Maria, enjoyed riding horses and owned several. Shawn opened the Saddle Shop to defray expenses of this sport.

When Maria left for college in Brandon, Virginia her mother left with her. Later that same year Shawn's wife purchased one hundred acres of undeveloped land outside of Brandon using most of their joint savings account without consulting Shawn. Since that money was for their retirement, Shawn assumed she wanted them to retire there. Every vacation he went south to develop the land with a large manufactured home and patio plus drive connected to the road.

Then he dug ponds, established trails and generally improved the large tract. When Maria graduated from college, Shawn established a saddle goods shop in Brandon for them to run and stocked it at his own expense to get the business started without debt. He assumed that when he retired, he would join them down there. However, when he finally mentioned that to his wife, she told him he was not welcome and wanted a divorce. What's more, she wanted half of what he had in River City as well as everything in Brandon. They were still haggling over terms when Shawn and I met. When the case went to court, the judge decreed she could have either what was in Brandon or what was in River City, not both. She, of course, settled for the larger portion in Brandon.

At last, his divorce finalized, we worked out a careful contract under which I rented a bedroom and study which included access to the bathroom and kitchen…actually the whole house and yard… for a set amount plus specified chores. It was a grand arrangement for two lonely but marriage-shy adults.

Financially, I made headway on clearing up my child-rearing debts on several credit cards. They represented birthdays, holidays and vacations which needed to be celebrated in addition to basic food, clothing, and shelter. Although my ex-husband paid medical, dental, and music lessons in order to claim his children as dependents, the strain on my single salary was extreme. I even took on teaching a Creative Writing Course for additional income.

Long deferred maintenance like a new roof kept me from large profits as a landlord. One really needs several properties to cover "down time" between tenants. It also helps if one is handy at repairs. Ron gave me a self-fixer's manual one Christmas, but I was not very adept nor did I have the tools for all but simple tasks like hanging a picture or tightening a screw. I wound up imposing upon handy friends like Shawn or incurring bills from a handyman service.

Since no building permit had been obtained for converting the garage into a "cottage", I eventually ran into official displeasure when a deadbeat tenant had the nerve to complain to the Health Department about the quality of the water at the cottage. The health and building inspectors descended. I had to forcibly evict the cottage's tenants and, tired of all the hassles, I put the Refuge up for sale. Standing on your own doorstep begging for the rent several times each month until at least a portion was paid was onerous.

Even after listing the property for sale there were problems—the appraiser marking the value down because my "outbuilding" was neither garage nor legitimate apartment. A nice couple made a fair offer on the cleaned up place, but after two weeks their first-time buyer mortgage was not approved ... something about the wife's changing jobs too often.

If Shawn hadn't forgiven me three months' rent during the selling period, I'd have had to file for bankruptcy due to mortgage payments, second appraisals, well testings (three before we passed), lawyers' fees for eviction proceedings, yard upkeep, continuing utility and phone costs, etc. What had begun as a great adventure in self-sufficiency, theoretically possible, wound up more a burden than a blessing. While the children were at home, the experiment racketed along with their help, but the toughness of a landlord needing to make a profit did not coincide with my caring, mild nature. Almost anyone else could have told the newly hired River City College soccer coach with six children that my place was just too small for that size family. Not me. For a year I tried to pacify the unhappy wife's complaints about the hardness of the water, the dampness of the basement, the fences' needing repairs, the leaves in the eaves troughs, etc., etc. They moved to a four-bedroom home north of town after that academic year.

The single-again young salesman liked being near the public golf course, but he complained that the clothes in his closet reeked of mildew. A short reconciliation with his ex-wife went poorly and eventually he moved to a new apartment complex without the "huge yard."

Despite some nostalgia for the good times my brood had experienced in the "Retreat," it was with great relief I signed final closing papers with a family whose two teenaged sons would be living in the converted garage.

CHAPTER TEN

Finally Finding Security

Having given up on the advice in <u>One Acre and Security</u>, the four children now raised and educated, the debts entailed liquidated by the property sale, I began to look forward toward retirement. Several church members had suggested I train to become an ordained deacon in the Episcopal Church. After all, I had served two separate terms as senior warden besides stints as organist, flower chairman, acolyte, and member of the Bishop's Committee. Although few thought it would succeed, I had written a grant proposal to fund building a parish hall for St. Stephen's and the national church had indeed funded our expanded building. This resulted in congregational growth with additional room for outreach programs.

In cooperation with a regional non-profit we were enabled to host a day care and lunch program on weekdays for elderly which permitted their caregivers to hold paying jobs. St. Stephen's bore housing costs and provided volunteers for lunch duty while the charity supplied paid professional staff.

I'd also—after serving six years on the CHEC (Cranston Episcopal Cursillo) governing board—told the Lord I'd be open to new outreach ministry. "Almost anything except prison ministry. I don't think I'd be any good at prison ministry." NEVER DARE THE LORD!

Two weeks after that prayer I received a phone call from the Pearl City Roman Catholic Cursillo. They were planning a weekend in the prison twenty miles south of River City and wanted someone local on their team. My name had been suggested. I never discovered who recommended me, but I agreed to serve. For three Sunday afternoons I traveled to Pearl City to train with their team.

The evening of the second day of the prison Cursillo), at the motel where we spent nights, the leader approached and told me why they'd wanted a local person on their team. They had received permission to hold Saturday afternoon Bible studies as a followup to this Cursillo Weekend. The distance from Pearl City was too far for their people, so I was to organize and provide the Bible studies. That was how River City Prison Fellowship began.

Initially I called in favors from local Episcopalian clergy and lay people, but learned that the jail ministry in River City was overcrowded and fundamentalists were actively looking for ways to fulfill Christ's Biblical instruction to visit prisoners. The Saturday afternoon Bible studies at the prison filled the bill and before long we had enough volunteers that most of them only had to drive the twenty miles once a month to provide music and lessons from the same study guides.

One reservation applied—their women couldn't go to an all-male prison. The Lord responded by having the State of Indiana add a women's compound to the prison. Naturally, the women prisoners requested they also be provided Saturday afternoon Bible studies. River City Prison Ministries responded by having two teams going down each Saturday afternoon with women only for the second Bible study.

As with any ministry organized with God's help, I turned River City Prison Fellowship over to other leaders as soon as it was well established. That way I couldn't be tempted to claim ownership because any ministry always belongs to the Lord.

A first I rejected suggestions about the diaconate, certain I would never be accepted for training with two divorces in my background, much as I would love to better serve the gracious Lord who had answered so many of my desperate prayers and brought me and my dependents through so much. Finally, to quell the increasing pressure, I agreed to submit my application and put an end to their ill-founded hopes I could become a deacon. However, my six years with the Cursillo Commission and later serving as secretary to the

Diocesan Search Committee that brought Bishop Grantham to Cranston were evidently well regarded by the headquarters staff in Cranston. To my shocked surprise a letter arrived stating that I had permission to become a candidate for the diaconate.

The subsequent procedures were long and elaborate-recommendations from my home church, costly physical and mental evaluations, attendance at an information conference, and at last- interviews at a retreat held at Mercy Foundation in Ripon, Wisconsin.

I was familiar with Mercy Foundation having attended several retreats there. I liked its spacious lawns and gardens, gymnasium with swimming pool, stone Victorian chapel utilized for weddings plus receptions in the activity building. I used to pray beside the raised stone sarcophagus of Blessed Justin Denforth outside the Chapel. It was unnerving to be at this culminating event at the close of which I would either be accepted or rejected for diaconal training. Of the first two interviews, I was encouraged by the positive attitudes shown by the questioners. My third interview, however, was conducted by a clergyman who was a close friend of my ex-husband, Fr. Patrick. I detected or at least suspected some animosity on his part and my hopes crashed.

Not wanting to run into anyone after I left that last interview room, I went outside and over to Denforth 's tomb in tears. Softly, but aloud, I said, "I don't believe I'm going to get to be a deacon."

To my amazement, a male voice responded, "Of course you will become a deacon." I looked all around, but no one was near. "Pluck the rose beside you," the same voice instructed. Beside the grave was a rose bush with a single blooming white rose.

'Oh, Blessed Justin, it is the only and last one on your bush," I demurred, for it was early November, late for roses.

"The rose is for you and so are the thorns," the voice concluded.

I've never heard that voice again although I've been to Mercy Center numerous times since. Nor has there ever been another rose bush by that grave. As he predicted, I was indeed included as one of the seven successful candidates at the final service. I dried and pressed the rose. It is in one of my prayer books.

The next communication regarding my studies for the diaconate deflated my optimistic balloon. The program was on hold for a year while it was being revised. Those revisions were extensive—three years instead of two years of commuting to alternate all-day Saturday classes in the Cranston area. The worst news was that the Diocese of Cranston would no longer underwrite the cost of our studies. We were advised to plan on $10,000 for tuition and study materials. Where in the world could I find $10,000?

I sat down sadly to write a thanks-but-no-thanks letter back to the Archdeacon. After six faltering drafts, this Creative Writing instructor discerned that I was not intended to reject this diaconal training. Accordingly I turned it all over to the Lord. "You'll have to help me find the money if You want me to become Your deacon," I pleaded. And He did—not all at once, but just enough and often from unexpected places.

Another complication to becoming a deacon was that my new female vicar of St. Chad's stated that unless Shawn and I got married or I moved out of his home into single housing, she would not approve my application. Then I explained this requirement to Shawn and when a proposal for marriage was not forthcoming, paid a deposit on an apartment near River City College.

I had arranged to have my piano moved over to the apartment when Shawn called work late one morning to inquire if I could be free to have lunch with him. This was very unusual, but I agreed to meet him at Burger King at eleven forty-five. When we met, I noticed immediately that he was not in work clothes. After obtaining our orders, we slid into a booth across from one another and began to eat.

"Whatever is the occasion?" I inquired.

"Well, it's not every day I ask someone to marry me," he responded. "Yes or no?"

"You waited until after I'd made arrangements to move to ask me? I might have to think it over."

"Somehow I didn't realize how much I'd miss you." This was a gigantic statement for a man of few romantic words. It echoed my own feelings, so I didn't keep him waiting any longer. "Yes," I said.

"Yes, you'll marry me? Thank God, Lara. You'll never be sorry," he promised as he grabbed one of my hands and kissed it. In the parking area we sealed our new relationship with a huge hug and lingering kiss. Then we both returned to our jobs and I phoned to cancel moving plans.

That night we agreed to be married in the River City College Chapel by the Methodist Chaplain rather than seek permission from the Episcopal Church. Then we could have my vicar bless our union after one year had passed.

My family and best friend attended the simple wedding ceremony and the luncheon afterwards. We had satisfied the vicar's condition- the last of the many obstacles to my becoming a deacon.

Marriage to Shawn resolved my emotional difficulties, too. His loving support for my plans to become a deacon after retiring from River City College meant so much to me. All my children liked Shawn and approved our marriage. At last I felt secure with God and whatever the future might hold.

EPILOGUE

The future included retirement from River City College after twenty-five years as a professor, ordination as a Deacon in the Cranston cathedral, and moving to Florida with Shawn. Since my home church in Lonely Park did not want to lose me, they designated me as their missionary to Florida. Accordingly, I chose a startup Episcopal mission of the Diocese of Central Florida to serve as deacon. They have grown to become a parish with over 300 members, substantial buildings, and numerous outreach ministries.

My own writing has resulted in three collections of poetry and one novel being published. This account is recorded in the hope that it may encourage other single parents and in gratitude for how gracious God has been. All four of my children are solid citizens, hard workers, and trustworthy adults despite the tortuous paths we endured together getting there.

Printed in the United States
By Bookmasters